D1575297

THE ROAD TO FAITH

Books by Will Oursler

FATHER FLANAGAN OF BOYS TOWN (with Fulton
  Oursler)
NARCOTICS: America's Peril
THE PRUDENTIAL
THE BOY SCOUT STORY
THE HEALING POWER OF FAITH
FROM OX-CARTS TO JETS
LIGHT IN THE JUNGLE (Editor)
THE ROAD TO FAITH

and many novels

Will Oursler

THE ROAD TO FAITH

Holt, Rinehart and Winston
New York

Grateful acknowledgment is made to the following publishers for permission to reprint excerpts from their publications:

OXFORD UNIVERSITY PRESS, INC., New York, N. Y., for permission to reprint excerpts from DIALOGUES OF PLATO, translated by Benjamin Jowett; and

CHARLES SCRIBNER'S SONS, New York, N. Y., for permission to reprint excerpts from HEADS AND TAILS by Malvina Hoffman.

"Wilkie Was Army," which appears on page 165, first appeared in the August, 1945, issue of *True*.

Published, March, 1960
Second Printing, June, 1960

In Canada, Holt, Rinehart and Winston of Canada, Limited

Copyright © 1960 by Will Oursler
Printed in the United States of America
All rights reserved
Library of Congress Catalog Card Number 60: 5227

To Fulton with love

Author's Note

This book is written not for those who have found faith, but for those who seek it, or who wonder if they could ever learn truly to believe in any religious creed.

It does not deal in terms of doctrine as taught by any individual religion; yet it seeks to present certain basic truths found in all faiths.

It does not offer final answers, but only possible beginnings. It tries to approach the religious experience not in organizational but in personal terms, the terms of life and its people and its stories, its hurts and needs, defeats and triumphs.

It does not oppose any religion or sect, or plead the cause of any individual denomination. I am sure that theologians who read this book will forgive the discursive lack of a dogmatic position; my purpose is not to deal with fine points of theology but only to help some who are questioning to come perhaps a little closer to the goal, to the aura of faith.

For the rest—the goal—the journey itself—lie in the heart and the spiritual hunger of the reader.

WILL OURSLER

Contents

THE ROAD TO FAITH

A Word in Advance

For each of us there is the mountain, and its road of faith, the crags and crevasses, the plunging cliffs, the sudden vistas and outreaching horizons. And each of us, young and old, artist or scientist or businessman, must find his own pathway to his still uncharted stars.

The challenge of the road—the issues—the decisions—are inescapable. For we must live as though a universal consciousness we call God, a power of meaningful purpose, to Whom we can turn, is a fact or is not, exists or does not, is or is not. The meaningful character of our lives, or the lack of it, is the core of the question. We cannot avoid an answer; we cannot hope to remain contented for a lifetime—or longer—perched in indecision on a cosmic fence.

The mountain is a way, a goal, an achievement. It is an awareness and synthesis of the whole that gives reason and meaning to the particular.

The mountain is the summation of an infinity of purposes blended into individual purpose and fulfill-ment; it is the culmination of ourselves and the surmounting of our weakness; it is the searching out of ourselves in the inner fortress of being; it is an expedition none but we may pursue, a road none but we can follow, a reconnaissance in force of the soul.

The road is for those who seek, those who are unsure, those who grope. The mountain way, in fact, is an ever-continuing process; we gain the goal only to lose it, to slip back, to regain it once more, stronger and more certain than the last time.

There are those who believe, unquestioningly, unequivocally—not only Christians and Jews, but Moslems and Buddhists, Taoists and Hindus; the faithful are found in every great religion. None has any right to question the sacred implications of another's faith. For them there is no search; they have accepted unconditionally.

There are others who seek, but who at the same time are afraid. They fear self-deception and wishful thinking. They seek the truth on its own terms, without equivocations, sentimentalism, evasion, cliché in place of sound reason; they want the right to probe, to question, to doubt, to disbelieve, to refute and reject as well as to accept.

Too often these seekers are turned away from any role in organized religion by the overpowering importunities of well-meaning "believers" who insist on their own special avenues of faith above all the rest.

Too often those who do hunger after holiness are turned back from the mountain road by high walls of complicated and sometimes outmoded theology that they cannot accept, by emphasis on ritual and formalism rather than faith itself, by the religious zealot who rushes in with his arguments—and his condemnation of all who believe otherwise—as if he alone had all the answers.

Seekers on this mountain road usually have no such certainties. They are full of their question marks and dossiers of doubt, their logic and lack of it, their misunderstandings and misinformation. Why should we be called sinners? they demand. What is meant by the guilt of the human race, the fall of man? If Unitarians are wrong, are Lutherans right? If Catholicism is right, do Jews spend eternity in hell? And what of the Buddhists? Why does the ministry keep denouncing humanity as wicked and sinful and debased? We refuse to believe that we are debased, sinful and lost, they insist. Why are we guilty, all of us? What kind of God would condemn His children as guilty, the way some radio preachers and churchmen shout and bemoan and lament?

Any attempt to answer these questions would be meaningless, in any case, if the questioner is without the religious experience. One can talk of the individuality of faith and its interpretations and complications—and all of these things must by their very nature be individual—but one cannot substitute argument for reality, compulsion for willing surrender, shabby emotionalism for the actual experience of God.

§ 15 §

Beginnings are difficult and groping. We worry at the start over nonessentials and almost dismiss the heart of truth. Long ago, I remember, I gave a talk to a men's group at a church on why so many Americans did not go to church or support any organized faith.

I had marshaled all the reasons: the failure of organized faith to keep up with the times, with science and psychology; the failure of major religions to agree among themselves; the hypocrisy of so many in church activities—the backbiting of the committee ladies, the pettifogging technicalities of many in the clergy, the concern of church authorities too often with running a big business rather than with religion itself.

I cited in this talk the difficulty of finding the religious experience in the midst of so much spiritual confusion and seeming contradictions. I pointed out that those seeking reality turn and run in instinctive revulsion before the untempered imprecations of men whose metaphysical concepts make no sense and have no impact on the individual as against the impact of modern psychology, or biochemistry, nucleonics or astrophysics.

They should have been angry or annoyed at that talk of mine. I stated what I then believed firmly, and pulled no punches. Yet from their questions I caught no anger, hurt, resentment, or anything of the kind. They were curious; they were interested in this group of the unchurched of whom I spoke. They seemed to be saying: "What a shame that these people do not understand. And how can you help us to help them?"

I was startled at this reaction. It came to me as I listened to the questions in the discussion period that this group of believing men had wellsprings of strength I had not suspected at all.

The truth was that they had no fear of questions, of doubts, of discussions about rituals and dogmas and the weaknesses of humanity and particularly of committees, and the frailties of individuals in church and out.

They had no fear, I realized, because they knew. They had found their way.

There was a time when faith was on the forbidden list—socially. It was bad taste to discuss religion in the drawing room. Today we are not afraid. The issues have become too immediate and important in our lives.

Our world has become a community; we know each other in a new way; Mohammedan and Jew and Christian are neighbors and brothers and what happens to one may happen to all; the word is flashed with the speed of light around the globe. The brotherhood of all men begins to assume the reality of experience on a world-wide basis.

Already this brotherhood begins to probe space itself. The dome of heaven is no longer a glass bowl pinpricked with stars; it is an ocean of unknown reality to explore.

§ 17 §

The answer to what lies beyond the stars will one day be found in terms of telescopes and nose cones, and our prespacial, earth-oriented theologies must fit the unfolding facts of a universe that belongs—we may be certain—not to us alone.

Thus in whatever direction we look—to philosophy, religion, science—or to ourselves—the challenge and the adventure of a living faith awaits.

It is that challenge—that road—we pursue here.

When one sets out upon a journey, it is usual to bring along maps and pamphlets, designed to aid the traveler by pointing out places of interest and warning of congested areas and possible detours, at the same time painting the enchantment of the district: "The city mirrors the charm of the sunlit landscape rolling out on all sides; the very streets follow the routes of mountain streams long vanished under the cobblestones. . . ."

But there are different kinds of journeys; there are pilgrimages of varied purpose, to divergent destinations. The itineraries of some are elusive; there are a thousand maps and none alike; a thousand would-be guides, each claiming exclusive rights to the road, insisting that they alone know the way. And the hazards of such itineraries sometimes lie beyond the range of familiar frontiers.

To some, above all to the agnostic and atheist,

the promise and perils of a journey into faith are mere phantoms, an emptiness of words, lacking the solidity of the tangible, the reality of the molecular.

A warning is needed, however: Those who start upon an exploration into faith must be prepared to face whatever reality they encounter, even if that reality is not as easy to grasp, as tactile or comfortable, as our familiar, everyday patterns, our shopworn prejudices and ideas.

The seeker must at least be aware of the possibility of realities beyond the sensory; he must be prepared to listen to promptings within and beyond himself. He must learn to accept the experience without imposing his own will upon it, lest the experience elude him completely or have no meaning.

The quest—the mountain road—is for all who seek. It is for the believer who doubts and the disbeliever who begins to question his own disbelief. It can have meaning for those who have begun to travel their own road, but even more for those who have lost their way or reached an impasse; for the afraid or bewildered; for the curious and the beguiled; for those who wonder, in the midst of aloneness, if there could be a road for them; for those who long to believe and cannot, who seek a path through the wilderness of their disbelief.

Only two facts about this search for faith are sure.

One is that the quest itself can be the great adventure of our lives.

And the other is that God is there, if we dare to venture far enough over ways we have not gone before.

1

CATALYST

How and why do we begin this search? For each person the moment is unique. To some it comes in victory, achievement, gratitude; to others in an abyss of sorrow; to one in loss, in bewilderment; to another in sudden, wordless surmise.

Triumphant or searing, out of today or yesterday, or remembered from the dust-ridden past, the moment serves a catalytic purpose when we grasp—at last—its deeply personal meaning.

It becomes then a point of departure for any who yearn to discover—or perhaps to rediscover—a way to faith.

The ringing of the phone arouses me. I get up to answer it in the gray half-light of dawn. The voice of my sister, April, tells me that my father has suffered a heart attack.

He is resting now, she is saying. They have given him drugs for the pain. The doctor is with him. She will call me back in moments.

I dress quickly. In the quiet, my wife and I wait. In the other room my own son sleeps. The clock ticks noisily.

Then the phone again. My sister's voice is telling me to come at once; there is no time.

The apartment in the hotel on Central Park South is silent. It is a terrible silence, a silence that seems to shout. It fills the rooms with the roar of its noiselessness.

As I come into this place, the hush of its sweeps through me. So much is in this apartment, so much between my father and me that none but we can understand, so much flooding my consciousness, without words or deliberate thought. So much that needed no words, for it was part of a lifetime, part of the roots of our existence.

In how many ways do father and son know each other? In how many special ways do they test themselves and their ideas, one against the other? In how many ways are they bound together with the special steel of their father-son relationship? How many times does one insist upon his point, his way, one moment, only to surrender it the next? How many times does a grin and a handshake erase anger and hurt? How often do they teach without knowing they teach, learn without realizing they learn—from each other?

My father and I were friends. It was far more than parent and offspring. We shared a world of excitement, a universe of new ideas and discoveries and challenge. We argued and debated and disagreed and even quarreled sometimes, and we made up as we always knew we would. We roamed the world with our ideas and tired the night with our talk.

What can one say about a father one loved? What can one think at such a moment, walking into the almost unearthly hush of that modern New York apartment?

There was so much people didn't know: the warmth of his life and his interests that galloped from philosophy to modern physics, from crime and its solution to magic and ventriloquism, from the mysteries of the ancient Egyptian tombs and the drama of the French Revolution to the taste of fog and the smell of the sea.

No one could tell a tale with quite his enthusiasm. Whatever he touched took on the aura of his special excitement, his intensity. His life was a multicolored tapestry of many scenes and motifs.

A magician in his youth, he was somehow a magician all his life. Like a stage prestidigitator, he could turn the commonplace into rare treasure, the empty water glass into a vase of wondrous flowers.

He loved to laugh, to tell a story, to find the unexpected turning, to touch the heart of his listeners. I remember a story he related of his own youth, when he was a seventeen-year-old reporter on a Baltimore newspaper, and just married to my mother.

One morning his managing editor asked him, "Fulton, do you play any musical instrument?"

The answer was no.

"Do you sing in your church choir?" the editor persisted. "Or sing at all? Or know anything at all about music?"

"No, sir."

"Good! You are the new music critic of this paper."

And then Fulton would tell us how he attended his first concert that night, as a critic, a concert by the great violinist, Fritz Kreisler. Fulton listened entranced, but with little idea of what he should say in his first official critique.

As the concert was ending, he hurried backstage and requested an interview with the musician. Kreisler agreed. In the dressing room, the seventeen-year-old critic explained the situation frankly.

It was his first such assignment, he said. And he had no right to be a critic at all, because he knew little about music except that he loved it.

"Mr. Kreisler," he said, "if you were writing an objective review of your concert tonight, what would *you* say about it?"

The musician was beguiled. He walked up and down the dressing room and began to consider each number he had played, what was right, what was wrong, what went well and what did not. The bowing in the opening selection, he stated thoughtfully, seemed perhaps a little careless. But the cadenza in the next went very well indeed. . . .

When his story appeared, Fulton liked to recall, none on the newspaper staff could quite understand how he had learned so much about music in so short a time.

Fulton continued as music critic on the paper and later came to New York as editor of a music magazine. He learned a great deal about music and loved to sing arias from operas, especially as he dressed and shaved in the morning.

But that morning in the apartment there was no song or sound.

Some things I did not and could not share with him. I remained a Protestant when he became a Roman Catholic. The family on both my father's and mother's side were Protestant, and even though my faith was at best nominal, at the same time I did not wish to run to something else I knew and understood even less.

But I was glad for him. For his religion gave him a true rebirth; his life took on new meaning, new direction, new fulfillment. For Fulton there was no longer doubt, questions or searching.

Once when we talked of the confusions and contradictions of our time, he told me, "But I am not living in this time only, Bill, I am living in eternity."

All of the past, all of our lives, even those words of his, flashed across my own consciousness in the hush of that morning, as I came into the apartment.

I opened the door into the bedroom. I saw my father lying there and I knew that he was dead and I fell to my knees and hid my face with my hands.

The silence goes on, lives on, in different ways. The silence of the voice you do not hear again. The silence of the long hours in the night. The silence of questions for which you find no answers.

In what does one believe? What remains when the man is gone, not only of his work but of himself? Did Fulton live in eternity as he so certainly believed? Was personal survival a fact, an objective, a necessity? Or did bonds of love rot with the skeleton in the earth?

We had been so close and yet I could not accept life or death or faith in the terms he had come to accept. But was his approach to universal truth possibly true in his terms, or in mine, whatever they were (and I did not then know for sure), or in any terms at all?

Out loud in the dark I asked my question, but in the darkness I heard no voice.

The silence goes on, days and months and even years. The silence of the unanswered; the gnawing, destroying silence within us; the emptiness of silence that hears no word of reply; the silence of the bereft who are not comforted; the silent treading of our doubts; the silence of the authoritarian's answer to our need, the formalized answer that cannot bend to the individual. Or so it seemed to me.

Yet answers I had to have. This I knew. Answers that meant something, answers that did not dodge my need, my demand, my logic, my awareness of modern science, my common sense. The universe was stable and meaningful and good, or it was a hideous, ugly bleeding crime.

There could be no middle ground, no neutrality on this point. One or the other had to be true, and I had to know.

And where and how did one begin to know?

Somehow I was aware, without knowing how, that my search must begin not across the vast wilderness of infinity, but within the finite boundaries of myself.

The way is of the spirit, of the infinite and eternal, but our grasp of it must filter through our own mortal being.

The channels to the Kingdom are open to us only when we learn to recognize them and accept them as such within ourselves.

And this contact is made in the wordlessness of understood need, of surrender, of search itself.

2

THE MOUNTAIN

We find God—and our faith in Him—not in words alone, or credos repeated, but above all in action and in awareness.

Awareness that is a conscious action, an inner seeking.

Awareness of the possibility of God as an active force in our lives.

Awareness that if God in His love created all things, we as a part of creation are also an object of His love, His readiness to respond when we turn to Him.

Awareness that such a divine love and power must work in ways beyond our finite understanding.

What and when is a coincidence?

It is not always possible to say.

Here is a dark, wind-swept road in Vermont, cutting across the Green Mountains. Fog and wisps of clouds drift over the black-top highway. Suddenly, with no warning, the car stops. The engine will not turn over. The lights work and everything else seems in order. But the car will not go.

The driver and his wife are alone. There are no houses nearby. Few cars pass this way at night—particularly on a night like this. Driving along the highway, the couple had not encountered another car for an hour.

But now, only moments after their car breaks down, another car appears. The man and his wife cry out for help. The oncoming vehicle halts.

Its two occupants are salesmen for an insurance company. One of them was a B-24 pilot in World War II. He was shot down over Germany, parachuted to safety and, with the aid of the German and French underground, traveling by night across enemy territory, made his way from one refuge to the next, until he reached the Channel and an underground ferry service that took him back to England.

Many people—men, women and children—at great personal risk, helped this man in his flight across Germany and northern France. And, as he explained to this young couple, he is grateful for every chance to help someone else who might be lost or stalled somewhere in the dark.

In his car he keeps chains and hooks, flashlights and other emergency equipment—everything necessary to tow this stalled car safely through the fog and mist to the nearest town, twenty miles away.

It is easy to call it coincidence, a fortuitous act of luck.

But those who have had such an experience many times, under many varying circumstances, might hesitate to dismiss its meaning so quickly.

For there is protection when we are not aware of it, even when we do not knowingly, consciously, ask for it.

And there are guides—and road maps—for each of us.

As a young boy—when I was nine or ten, I read adult books and novels from the open shelves of the library. Some made deep impressions upon me.

One concerned a man who drank too much. He ran away to South America and in the mountain wilderness encountered a hermit who gave him a philosophy of life. He was never supposed to repeat that philosophy twice over in the same words, but each time was to phrase it differently, being thus compelled to seek its meaning. "Each man," he might say on one occasion, "has the right to his own horizon, to see as far as he can see, to vision, to dream, to believe, to attain."

Or again he would put it: "We go as far as we can go. We do not measure ourselves by others but by our truest selves, the self of the innermost being." Or again: "We climb, each as high as he is able; each seeks his own way. We do not try to force our path upon another, but rather to help our brother find his way, as he helps us to find ours."

I do not recall the name of the book or its author. The words of the hero, as he fought his way back to his own world, as he scaled his own mountain—are not accurate phrase for phrase, but they are the essence of the words.

Words and meanings do not vanish entirely but linger in the side-street shadows of our mind.

To see as far as we can see. To reach beyond ourselves. To dare to search, to dare even to believe. To dare to climb as high as we have strength and vision to climb.

The goal is in the distance, a high challenge in the bright summer sun.

From my study window, far off, beyond the new green of the near fields and the darker green of trees on the long sloping hill behind the fields—beyond these is the mountain, pale gray against the sky.

It is a jagged mass of contradictions. Changeless, it changes constantly. Inanimate, it has special animation. Its contours are familiar as the face of a friend, yet differ from one moment to the next, now half lost in fog or rain, now sharp-outlined against a cloudless blue sky. A hunched mass against the dawn, or a sunset spectacle, tinted with gold.

To gaze upon the mountain is to dream. We must dream before we begin the journey, turning inward to our needs, our loneliness and our desires, and outward to our hopes. The distant gray-green pattern against the sky is a factor in all. For the mountain is the challenge and the security, the storm and the refuge.

Is there a road ahead, and how and where do we reach it? Is what we seek a concrete high-speed thruway? Or is it a narrow, unpaved path, twisting a route up the sheer side of the mountain? Or must we hew our own road, step by step and rock by rock, across crevasses and fissures and razor-edged ridges?

There is a saying among climbers that men scale mountains because they are there. It may be equally true in a metaphysical sense. We seek the road, and whatever danger-filled course it follows up the high slopes, because the far-off goal is there and we hunger to reach beyond ourselves.

We stumble on reasons that we may not understand; the goading force may come from promptings within us, intuitions that speak unbidden from grief or loss, turmoil or defeat, victory that proves empty. The mountain is there, and its challenge. We turn to other things but the challenge stays; overpowering implications tantalize the mind, in our secret moment, in our hidden weakness.

We tell ourselves that we are exaggerating the significance. There is no spiritual meaning beyond our own brain cells. The mountain is mere topsoil and rock, igneous masses pushed up by heat and gas into the sedimentary stratifications, so that the layers are flung back and twisted and overturned by the up-thrusting force. Geologists write history in terms of pressures, upthrusts, intrusions, great batholiths, earth revolutions and erosion; it is mechanistic and chemical and has nothing to do with humanity or the soul. The mountain is a mole on the face of the world; it has given a little and wrinkled a little, over a hundred million years, since the death of the Mesozoic and the dawn of the Cenozoic or modern era.

The history is all true and it is all, in another sense, false. For the ghostlike gray mountain looms beyond the hills and for each of us it is forever; the challenge and the meaning is forever, and the road is forever there.

The mountain is for dreaming and hoping and remembering—and for daring. Above all for daring. But to dare we must have the courage of the present; the mountain may be forever but the moment—and the courage—must be now.

For each of us there is the moment when we turn to the high path of faith. The reasons for turning, we have seen, are many: fear, uncertainty, loss, grief, sudden defeat and often—sudden triumph.

The moment may arise from awareness of beauty in the universe. It may find its beginning in the riddle of existence itself, when the unanswered seems to overwhelm us and we must achieve understanding or die.

One instant we do not care; the next we know only that we must know, we must begin this pilgrimage. We have no idea how we will find the road, or how difficult, or dangerous to our well-ordered lives, it will be.

We know only that it cannot be easy or safe and that only those who dare can learn what truth—if any —this mountain and its promise hold.

And so we set out for our road.

We seek a path to the mountain through a tangle of doubts and frustrations, unanswered questions, self-delusions.

For to find faith we must find meaning, to find meaning we must find reality, and to find reality we must seek God.

3

CARAVANS

The roads—and the caravans—are infinite.

Each approach is valid within its own dimensions.

No man can say how many avenues there are to God. The essential problem of the individual is to determine the road that is right for himself, for his special needs.

A preliminary step therefore is an orientation: Where do we begin? From what roots does our yearning for faith spring? From what spiritual point do we start?

And which road is there for us?

This much may be said: There are no new roads. They have all been traveled before, in different ways, over centuries. The road is not a single thing or a single way. There are many routes by which man walks, or limps, or crawls on battered hands, to faith. And it is not always easy to understand why one route appears so simple and the next so demanding.

For some it is a solitary journey; for others it is a caravan of friends and neighbors and family. Some make the journey in an aura of joy; some in terror; some in emptiness; others in curiosity. Some are driven by the surging needs of humanity.

Moses, leading the children of Israel out of Egyptian slavery; Moses obeying the word of God and leading the Jews across the desert to found a new nation—he was a man of such faith.

The story as told in the Bible is legend and philosophy and religion and myth and history interwoven into the great religious tapestry of the Pentateuch. Individuals differ in their interpretations of these accounts. Some accept them as factual, others as mere folklore, others as perhaps based in part on history. We may believe that the Red Sea parted, precisely as recounted, with the winds separating the waters and permitting the Jews to escape; we may reject all such events as unlikely.

But we cannot reject the figure of Moses, the leader, the man of faith, dedicating himself to his labors as a man of God, serving as a human implementation of Divine Will. We cannot reject this because reason and myth and history have nothing whatever to do with it; the humanity of Moses and of his faith swirls like a flooding tide across the centuries.

It was an elemental faith Moses brought. It was as basic and solid as the earth over which the ancient

Israelites trod, as real as the hot sun burning down upon them. Monotheism was still a new idea in the world; mankind was only beginning to grasp its implications. Jethro, father-in-law of Moses, cries out after their deliverance from the Egyptians:

"Now I know that the Lord is greater than all gods: for in the thing wherein they dealt proudly he was above them.

"And Jethro, Moses' father-in-law, took a burnt offering and sacrifices for God: and Aaron came, and all the elders of Israel, to eat bread with Moses' father-in-law before God."

The primitive concept of the burnt offering is transmuted by the deep sincerity of these men under the leadership of Moses. They sit with their offering not before pagan idols but before God.

They have no doubt of this for He has told them, "Thou shalt have no other Gods before me."

There is no question in their minds.

Yet the creed of that time was still elemental and even brutally harsh; life for life, eye for eye, tooth for tooth. Burning for burning, wound for wound, stripe for stripe.

Only with the later prophets of Judea came the broader concept of the God of love, of mercy, of forgiveness.

As with the individual, mankind also moves to faith, in its deepest and most meaningful sense, a step at a time.

But as we are all children of the same Father and part of the same creation, so true faith must reach across time, across lines of orthodoxy and denomination and individual sect. The names are not important. If there is one God to whom they pray, He is the same to all, He answers to all, He deals with all as the Father.

A man of Jewish faith and his wife and ten-year-old daughter were called to a town in Virginia to be with a dying relative who was alone in his last hours.

When they arrived, they learned that it might be days or weeks, this vigil. The parents were concerned about the little girl; they could not keep her with them constantly at the hospital, they did not want to leave her alone at the hotel.

Behind the hotel was a Lutheran church and school. A class of young girls played in the schoolyard below the hotel windows. The father of the ten-year-old went to the Lutheran minister, and explained his problem. They were an orthodox Jewish family, he told the minister; his little girl knew nothing of the Christian religion. But would it, perhaps, be possible for her to join with the other girls during their recess or playtime?

It was a small town; there were few Jewish people in this community. The minister knew how different would be the ideas and approach of the ten-year-old girl from the others.

Yet it was a challenge to him in terms not only of

brotherhood but of his own Christian ideals. The little Jewish girl, he told the father, of course could join with the others at playtime; why not also let her go into the classes at the school?

Out of this beginning came a time of learning. For apart from academic study, the ten-year-old learned also about the Christian faith and ideas, and the Lutheran girls learned to understand and respect the Jewish faith, as expounded by this little girl who had come into their midst.

In one session the ten-year-old told her classmates about Moses and the Ten Commandments and what these meant in her religion, as she had learned in her home and in her synagogue Sabbath school.

Each learned from the other, and each in the simple direct way of children accepted and respected and understood the other's way.

When finally the ten-year-old child went back north with her family, her proudest possession was her certificate of satisfactorily performed study in the Lutheran school.

No hatred—no prejudice—could ever destroy the meaning of this spiritual adventure to these children.

There are no new roads, we know, for faith is a thing within us, the faith of meaning rather than of outward symbol or name. Can we dare say that the faithful who bowed in true humility in the temple of a Roman or Greek god was not, indeed, praying to the Supreme Being as he understood that term? Can we say that his prayer could not be heard or answered by God?

The faithful of Islam make their caravan to Mecca and daily these nearly half billion true believers reiterate their creed: "There is no God but Allah and Mohammed is his prophet."

Are we to say that the road to faith does not exist for those who kneel five times daily facing toward Mecca, prostrating themselves to the ground before their God? Will the God they pray to reject them because the name is different from that in the prayers of the Christian-Judaic tradition?

Not a major religion holds such a view.

There is misunderstanding on this. Roman Catholicism, for instance, does not, as some mistakingly believe, teach that only Catholics go to Heaven. Within recent years, in fact, a Roman Catholic priest in Boston who preached such dogma was defrocked for heresy.

The "church universal," in the Roman Catholic concept, is composed of all who worship God according to the teaching to which they have been exposed, providing they live by what in objective standards could be called a decent moral code.

Each faith may cry and exhort and seek to convince others to its way. But none may dare to deny that other ways may also avail.

The gray-green sloping mountain that rises beyond the hills is there for all, and the roads are there for all. The caravans of humanity come to God by many routes.

The Japanese have a saying that there are many roads to the mountain, but those who reach the top look upon the same moon.

For Jesus the road was to Jerusalem and Pilate and Crucifixion. The human side of Jesus with its human frailties could have turned from the road. He knew what lay ahead in Jerusalem; yet He ordered the disciples to obtain him the colt of a donkey on which He rode into the city, fulfilling the prophecies.

"And a very great multitude spread their garments in the way; others cut down branches from the trees, and strewed them in the way.

"And the multitudes that went before, and that followed, cried, saying, Blessed is he that cometh in the name of the Lord:

"Blessed be the kingdom of our father David, that cometh in the name of the Lord: Hosanna in the highest."

He did not have to go into the city or the temple. Quite apart from any prophecies, it was obvious to all that the authorities were disturbed by the throngs Jesus was attracting, and were looking for a method to destroy Him.

Why, we wonder, in the midst of our prosaic

everydayness, did Jesus follow a road that He knew would lead Him to the agony of the Cross?

We grope for comprehension, we listen to sermons, we read books and explanations that contradict each other and seem bent upon compounding confusions in many instances.

Is there in the drama of the Crucifixion, we ask ourselves and the universe and the apologists of various creeds, the implication that we also must follow this road; that we must surrender to our enemies and to those who would destroy us, as He surrendered; that we, too, must bear our cross to a hill of skulls?

Is this the joyful news we are told to accept?

And if it is not, then what is the meaning?

Faith is an intimate and personal affair; yet at the same time it must be valid in the light of the reason and experience of the individual who seeks meaning in the universe. Mere surface acceptance is not faith; mere robot-repeating of empty phrases is not faith; willingness to conform is not faith; fear of being different or denounced as a heretic is not faith. Faith must be willing to stand the most minute and unbiased examination; the tenets of belief are the foundations on which the individual temple is built, and if they are molded of hypocrisy or mere social convenience, the temple will not stand.

"Spiritual hypocrisy" is one of the reasons cited by many who stay away from organized religion of any kind. Too often the hypocrisy they cite is actually only in their own minds, or only partially true. Human weakness besets us all; we talk of love even as we resent and hold prejudice, pride, or envy.

I once discussed this question of hypocrisy with a Baptist minister. His answer was to invite me to a special evening service at his church, which was to be conducted by another preacher.

We arrived a few minutes late. Perhaps our late arrival had been part of his plan. The entire congregation was on its knees praying, and rather than interrupt at that moment we stood at the back of the church. The minister leaned toward me and whispered a question, "Which of these people praying to God at this moment would you say is a hypocrite?"

I looked over this congregation of men and women and children bowed in the hush of a silent prayer. I could make no answer.

A child may ascend the road to faith along secure, familiar, well-traveled trails of family orthodoxy, accepting from earliest consciousness the particular faith of his parents, be it Christian Scientist or Protestant Episcopal, Roman Catholic or Taoist. To the child, this faith is real and unarguable; he accepts it as he accepts his meals, his bed and clothes. Later he may rebel and turn to other trails, but in his growing up the familiar trail is safe, and often the faith he finds on this road endures throughout his life.

Others travel the road in some traumatic hour where there appears no other way to go; it is this road or death. The climb is swift, in the midst of storm. The individual seeks safety, in a spiritual, not material sense. He seeks values beyond the intellectual, emotional, personal or philosophic. Out of such stormy adventure comes the sudden convert who, reaching **his** high keep of faith, clings to it and its validity like an embattled warrior defending the last outpost of the universe.

For some the point of departure is a vast desert of disbelief, rolling in barren glory to the edge of nothingness. There are those who begin their pilgrimage by insisting that the whole episode of religion is a mere stage in evolution, a wasted hour out of time. For them the journey is long and parched and plodding, across shifting dunes of doubt piled upon doubt.

Beyond these dunes—for any who travel that far —an awareness begins to come that disbelief is itself a faith, whether it is disbelief in one's own abilities or in the power of moral force or in God; disbelief is an act of faith, a positive stand. Disbelief in God involves a far-reaching decision about the universe, a decision that a Supreme Power does *not* exist, that the material universe is all, and that it made itself.

Many begin from this far-off point, driven by the need to justify the unjustifiable position of the agnostic or to prove the unprovable thesis of the atheist, compelled to wander across marshy acres of philosophical jargon, trying to get through the frustrating contradictions of so-called "realistic materialism." For example: If God did not make the universe, and there is no God-force or Power that did make it, then obviously it made itself. But this is unsatisfactory too; common sense says that *something* made something or there should be nothing at all.

The dilemma pursues the materialist like a hound; the more he runs the less sure he becomes, the less certain he can escape the logic that will not let him go. Whether he ultimately resolves the dilemma is a matter of the individual and his self-imposed limits.

The American philosopher, Hocking, writes: "The weakness of the realistic way of knowing is this: that in his preferential trust in analysis, the realist forgets that the human organ of knowledge is bi-focal, as befits a world in which the complex may be also simple. He has the right focus for the one but not for the other. If there are characters of the universe which are hidden from the wise and prudent and revealed unto babes, the realist will not find them."

The byways and blind alleys of half-truths or half-remembered dogma or half-forgotten scriptural text, tortured out of context to fit our own ideas, present a never-ending hazard.

How often do we run into the individual who tells us that he does not believe in church because he can worship God anywhere, in a barroom or in a grove of trees. But how often, we are tempted to ask, looking at him and his actions objectively, does he really worship God in a barroom or grove of trees—or anywhere?

There are those who say they worship God in doing good deeds and living a good life; isn't that enough?

But how often their definition of a good deed includes crushing an enemy underfoot—or a friend or a loved one—who stands in their way, in their light, for an instant too long?

Yet among the seekers and potential seekers are also those who, although almost or wholly unchurched, associated at best only vaguely with organized religion, still are looking for a faith that satisfies common sense and objective experience, rather than something they stumble into in a melodramatic aura of emotional storm.

For the millions who search in such terms, the answers must be as hard as steel and as self-evident and inescapable as death, taxes—and truth.

This is an army bewildered by claims and counterclaims, contradictions, disparities between what is said and what is done, the illogic of much in organized religion, the tenacious—often withering—hand of orthodoxy, the equally unrealistic and withering attitude of many intellectual realists.

These probing souls ask difficult questions and refuse easy answers. They ask about the Old and New

Testaments and the meaning of the Dead Sea Scrolls, about the age of the earth and the Fundamental position on the Garden of Eden, Adam and Eve, original sin and Noah's Ark; about evolution and biology and sex and modern psychiatry. They ask if God is to be feared or loved or both, and if He loves us, why should we fear Him?

They ask about modern living and killing and hating and the double talk of modern morality, and how these things square with the Bible and the Ten Commandments. They ask about the role of integrity in our daily lives and in our racial, social and international policies; they wonder at the righteousness of denouncing expediency when used by others and accepting it when used by ourselves.

Many of these millions are themselves part of what they question, the substance of their own doubts. They do not set themselves above the evils of which they are part; they seek rather to emerge from the evil, they seek a path. But wherever they turn, they find only the familiar duplicities and hypocrisies and dead ends. They run from the feudings and backbitings of the ladies in charge of the church bazaar; they shrink from the anti-Semites, the anti-Christians, the anti-Catholics one finds occasionally, even among some religious leaders. They wonder at the man who prays on bended knees in church but goes forth to spew out hatred of race or creed or political opponent, of laborer or business competitor, or against his wife or family, his own parents or children or brothers or sisters.

They form a strange army. They seek the road and they turn from roads that seem to mislead; they continue the search, losing the way and refinding it; recoiling and turning back and starting out again.

For these the journey is richest in promise.

For them, each step along the route, each slope and ridge and pile of frost-split rock that bars the way becomes an individual struggle, a triumph or defeat.

For these who seek, driven by hope and harried by doubt, the road presents questions that glitter in the distance, bright and unyielding and unequivocating as the high glacial ice.

4

OBJECTIVE

Why faith?

Is our goal merely adventure? Excitement? Curiosity? Or superiority—the knowledge that we are on our way while others are not, we are en route to salvation—while the unenlightened are on their way to nothingness?

Is it fear or hope, reason or emotion, need or nonsense?

The founder of Layman's Sunday is an advertising man. His agency is not like others. Much of its activity is freely given to causes of faith—to helping youngsters in trouble, to publicizing Layman's Sunday and other spiritual endeavors, to telling the story of modern Christian living to thousands of people through radio broadcasts, interviews and other similar methods.

On his advertising staff he employs one expert whose only job is helping this advertising company "witness" for Christ through various spiritual and so-cial-service activities.

This is a big Madison Avenue agency, with many hundreds of top commercial accounts. Why does this agency head go to such lengths? "Because I want to serve God on His terms rather than my own," is his answer.

He seeks to carry out what he feels is the will of God for him. "Our religious faith," he told me, "begins to work with our realization that God has a role for us, often far beyond what we believe possible."

The inner voice speaks, and we learn at last to lis-ten. The impulse comes and we do not push it away. The Presence comes in the silence, and we are aware. God speaks and we learn to hear His voice.

With the wisdom of intuition, we know it is His word; we know deep within ourselves.

Or if we do not believe, we are at last aware of possibility. This is the step—this awareness. This is a bridge that must be crossed at the start.

To reach infinitude, we begin with finite steps.

In the distance is the gray-green of the high mountain, beyond the low hill lands. Half clad in the soft haze, it is a thing of delicate beauty and terrifying challenge.

To climb it, to find a route upward to its dizzy and incomprehensible heights, is the goal we set.

The achievement is more than the mere ascent. It

is a soul-shaking experience; it changes our lives. It leaves its mark and its scars upon us. It is victory; it is a communion with the universe.

The achievement is accomplished by a variety of means in our modern world, exactly as any dangerous and challenging mountain is scaled. There are those who plan each detail with meticulous care; supplies, clothes, maps, provisions of all sorts against all possible contingencies. There are those who climb with no plans whatsoever; because it is a lark, because it is exciting, because it is for all or nothing. There are those who climb for duty and those who climb because only in this way can they find themselves; there are those who climb in weakness, and others in strength.

The reasons and the ways are as various, as complex, as ambivalent, as we ourselves.

Yet, once committed to the proposal, the mountain climber must pause to look ahead, to examine the problems he may encounter, the obstacles, the possible points of failure, of disaster.

En route to the beginning of the actual climb, he finds much that he as an individual has to reappraise; prejudgments and preconceptions must be discarded and altered to fit actual climbing conditions. From the moment he begins, the question pounds at him: How have I misunderstood so much?

There is so much that we must learn before the actual attempt to make the climb, about ourselves and the route ahead and the summit we seek.

§ 51 §

Whose faith, we ask, and in what?

It can be answered truthfully only in personal terms. Faith is within ourselves in a personal way because it can exist in no other. The airline hostess has no fear in a plane, but stands terrified before a wood stove in a farmhouse; the farm wife handles the stove without fear, but is terrified in a four-engine plane purring across the sky. Each is a measure of faith.

We may put our faith in sacred writings: the Bible, the Talmud, the Koran, the Pali canons; in the works of philosophers, sages, scientists. We may accept the statement of St. Paul that faith is the substance of things hoped for, the evidence of things unseen.

We may have faith in mystery, in miracle, in ritual, in moral code. We may accept some Oriental creed like that of Taoism—the word "Tao" itself meant "road" or "way" in its original sense. In Taoism emphasis is placed upon one main concept—returning good for evil. Lao-tse, its spokesman, gives three ways of applying this concept: through compassion, through moderation, through humility.

We may put our faith in a single command or injunction or affirmation. *Love one another.* Or: *Do unto others as you would have them do unto you.* Even: *Day by day in every way I'm growing better and better.*

William James, in his essay "The Will To Believe," insists that faith is, in part at least, a sign of courtesy to the universe, the will to accept it as a divine and beautiful and moral business, and not the happenstance of soulless, meaningless atoms, merging and dissolving like shadows in the night.

"Sad experience," he states, "makes me fear that some of you may shrink from radically saying with me, *in abstracto,* that we have the right to believe at our own risk any hypothesis that is live enough to tempt our will. I suspect, however, that if this is so, it is because you have got away from the abstract logical point of view altogether, and are thinking (perhaps without realizing it) of some particular religious hypothesis which for you is dead. The freedom to 'believe what we will' you apply to the case of some patent superstition, and the faith you think of is the faith defined by the schoolboy when he said, 'Faith is when you believe something that you know ain't true.' I can only repeat that this is a misapprehension."

But James also points out that a large area of what we believe is shaped by what we want to believe. "As a rule," he declares, "we disbelieve all facts and theories for which we have no use. Clifford's cosmic emotions find no use for Christian feelings. Huxley belabors the bishops because there is no need for sacerdotalism in his scheme of life. Newman, on the contrary, goes over to Romanism, and finds all sorts of reasons good for staying there, because a priestly system is for him an organic need and delight. . . .

"Evidentally, then, our non-intellectual nature does influence our convictions. There are passional tendencies and volitions which run before and others which come after belief. . . ."

Faith, the evidence and the authorities appear to agree, is no homogeneous substance, but a multiplicity of factors meshed together by the forces of our lives, by wind and storm, sun and moon and stars and cold; the freezing and congealing, the thrusting, knifing edges of pain and defeat, the high splendor of triumph, not over others but over ourselves.

Too often we find the answer only in a moment of extremity, when all other factors have failed; even here, we are inclined to doubt, to misinterpret what is happening. The miracle appears to be no miracle at all, but only a "working out" of the problem.

How often do we pray and have an answer and hear someone counter: "But wouldn't it have happened that way in any case, prayer or no prayer?"

A West Coast attorney dined one night with a client who was obviously deeply disturbed. After a prolonged silence, the client told the lawyer abruptly: "Tomorrow, Jim, I am going to kill myself."

The attorney realized his client was serious. It was no joke and no bluff. He suggested they order another drink and talk it over. The client agreed; nothing was going to alter his already determined course.

He was ruined financially. There was no other way for him.

They discussed the impending suicide quite objectively. Jim asked for particulars behind the financial crisis. "My business is wrecked," the client said. "I owe everyone and they are all after my neck. In a week I'll be in court. Bankrupt. My family disgraced. My name . . ."

It was no use talking to such a man about the sin of suicide, of taking one's own life, the gift of God, and destroying it. The client had no faith in God or himself or anything at all—except death.

But the lawyer explained to him that the suicide was simply needless. There was another way entirely. He began to talk in terms this distraught businessman could believe and accept. "We can call a meeting of your creditors. We can outline the problem. They're men of business; they want their money don't they?"

"But they're ready to tear me to shreds; they write me threatening letters. They have their lawyers call me."

"If we just bring them together with a plan, so they can be sure of getting something back instead of nothing—they won't try to stop that."

New hope began to come as the lawyer explained what they might do. Then suddenly it changed into a look of horror. "I've written my wife," the client said. "I told her what I was doing and why. I said I would be dead when she received the letter."

"You tear that letter up," the lawyer told him.

"I can't. I've mailed it already—an hour ago."

All his fear was in reverse. To begin again, as the lawyer had outlined, this man had to have a fresh start with everyone in his life, his wife included.

This way moments of bleak despair would be laid before her, at his open confession of his inadequacy to meet life. He did not want to begin again on such a note.

"I never want her to know. I never want her to find out I reached such a point. For a week I've been living away from home because of this situation."

After a moment, the lawyer said, "Never mind that. I can handle it. You're going back to your wife and we'll get this straightened out, but right now you stay where you are until you hear from me."

The following morning the lawyer went to the town where this man lived. He concealed himself in the bushes outside the home. When the postman arrived, the lawyer "just happened" to be going up the path at the same moment. Casually he told the postman at the foot of the porch steps, "You can give me the letters. I'm going right into the house."

The postman handed him the morning mail, watched the lawyer ring the doorbell and went on his way. He did not see the attorney hurriedly go through the handful of letters, pick out one he sought and slip it into his pocket—later to be destroyed.

§ 56 §

The wife never knew. The creditors who came together were delighted at the program of repayment. Not only did this work out as planned, but the man went on to achieve success he never dared believe possible. He had in actual fact been given a new life, as a result of the concern, the love and care of a fellow human being.

Where there is care, where there is action, where there is help given—there also is the handiwork of God.

For this man it meant a life reborn, reshaped, re-affirmed. It meant success that continued through the years. It meant happiness for himself and his family.

The near-suicide of a quarter of a century past was merely an unpleasant fragment out of a long-forgotten dream that his wife and children never knew.

In "The Will To Believe," James quotes Fitz-James Stephen: "We stand upon a mountain pass in the midst of whirling snow and blinding mist, through which we get glimpses now and then of paths which may be deceptive. If we stand still, we shall be frozen to death. If we take the wrong road, we shall be dashed to pieces. We do not certainly know whether there is a right one. What must we do? Be strong and be of good courage. Act for the best, hope for the best, and take what comes. If death ends all, we cannot meet death better."

This is a moment of courage and blind hope and

resignation. If there is nothing beyond, he says, then we have nothing to win or lose. So we do not need to worry at all.

But this, we must recognize, is not faith; it is no more than well-mannered hope. Faith that envisions itself whipped is not faith; if it can envision its defeat in advance, where and how could it exist as faith at all?

Is the mountain a moment or a lifetime or forever?

The answer is that we can have no halfway faith; we believe or we do not, we seek or we stand still.

It is not an argument in semantics; it is a break-through to truth.

It is a victory not of self, but of surrender of self.

It is not an answer to a few wavering doubts but an absolute certainty that exists in experience and in spite of all argument against it; it is the sublime unwavering certainty which Jesus said could move the mountains themselves.

5

THE ROAD TO FAITH

STORM

One great teacher is example.

The experience of others—and of our own lives—is there for us, a roadside stand of shining mementos.

We hold this one or that in our hand; we catch a glint in this, an illuminating fact in that.

The truth sparkles suddenly, with a bright, dazzling gleam, in some item that almost eluded our attention—a jewel, a story, a painting we admire.

Or in sudden storm.

Some years ago, in an East Fifty-seventh-Street art gallery, I discovered a picture of a ship in a heavy, moonlit sea; a sailing vessel with the balloon jib played out full and the mainsails puffed with the wind, and a hint of moonlight on the mast and on the wildness of the sea itself.

There was a primitive force in the painting, in naturalistic terms. The sea itself was there, and its changing savagery. The picture seemed to have special meaning to me. There was loneliness in it; loneliness that permeated water and moonlight and ship and sails, the loneliness of people, I thought, and their lives. This was a ship running through darkness and storm—destination unknown.

To me, at that young moment, it seemed to symbolize an individual life: coming out of darkness like that in this seascape, plowing toward darkness, and the hour was a blending of moonlit beauty and storm and uncertainty.

It was an unwitting and shallow interpretation, as I look back upon it now. But that was a moment of transition; the war was ended and the world had not yet grown used to peace. In the conflict I had participated as a war correspondent. I had seen men of far greater courage and bravery than I could ever hope to have give their lives in that conflict, to restore sanity and decency and peace to the world.

The names of the enemies and their creeds do not matter; they are always different and they are always the same, and perhaps the answer will come that we must first destroy the evil within ourselves before we can hope to destroy it in enemies beyond our borders. The "fascist peril" has since become an empty phrase; there are new perils, and new enemies, and there have been new wars.

But then I was quite young and this moonlit picture seemed to sum up so much of the meaning and the lack of meaning, the darkness and the light. Some days after I first saw that painting, I mentioned it to my father over one of our luncheons when we talked out our ideas.

Fulton seemed bemused by my somewhat grim interpretation of the painting I had seen. He did not accept my bleak postwar outlook. "A picture—even a painting—sometimes changes, as we look at it, as our own eyes change," he told me. "Besides, if it means that much to you, then you ought to have it, simply for its beauty as a work of art. Sometimes we need hyacinths for the soul."

He smiled and we talked of other things. The following day, the painting arrived at my apartment, a gift from my father.

For many years it has been a part of my life, and has meant far more to me than any ordinary painting. In its shadows and patterns, I have found, and still find, hidden lights; remembering our lunch and sometimes searching my own thoughts to see how this picture and its meaning has changed for me.

Some months after my father's death, I found myself gazing at the picture he had sent to me, and recalling his words when we talked about it.

A new import swept through me in my own sense of loss at the moment. We can seek new meanings, and look with new eyes.

It seemed then as if my thoughts were driven

from this picture to something quite different; an episode I had read about another ship and another storm.

"And there arose a great storm of wind, and the waves beat into the ship, so that it was now full.

"And he was in the hinder part of the ship, asleep on a pillow: and they awake him, and say unto him, Master, carest thou not that we perish?

"And he arose, and rebuked the wind, and said unto the sea, Peace, be still. And the wind ceased, and there was a great calm.

"And he said unto them, Why are ye so fearful? How is it that ye have no faith?"

We have the picture of these frightened disciples, terrified for their lives in the midst of tempest, as any of us would be. And we have the image of Jesus, unconcerned, asleep on a pillow in the after part of the ship.

The storm did not matter. They could not be harmed. It was not just a feeling, a hope, a let-come-what-may attitude. He *knew* that they were safe in the Father's protection.

When they come to Him in their terror, there is surely surprise in His question: "How is it that ye have no faith?"

The question tolls like a bell across the centuries. It reaches into every corner of our existence, into our fears, our hopes, our crimes, our divorce courts, our idiocies and our ulcers, into every moment of our present daily lives.

§ 62 §

6

CHILD OF GOD

An artist once told me, when I asked his advice about training my artistically gifted young son, "Wait until he is older. Do nothing now but let him draw and paint. You see, now he knows all he needs to know and the greatest teacher in the world could do nothing except make him unsure. The world will do that in other ways and then you can send him to art school. But not now when he knows more than his teacher can ever know."

Too often—as this artist tried to tell me—our sophisticated learning, our imagined wisdom and knowledge, are merely end products of our errors, our hypocrisies, our self-deceptions.

We have a vast store of information—but find ourselves empty of understanding, without which faith becomes mere meaningless jargon.

This is a key factor of our quest.

It is in the seeking of knowledge that we gain

*wisdom and in the seeking of understanding that
we gain faith.*

"At the same time," St. Matthew records, "came
the disciples unto Jesus saying, Who is the greatest in
the kingdom of heaven?

"And Jesus called a little child unto him, and set
him in the midst of them,

"And said, Verily, I say unto you, Except ye be
converted, and become as little children, ye shall not
enter into the kingdom of heaven.

"Whosoever therefore shall humble himself as
this little child, the same is greatest in the kingdom of
heaven."

And in another place Jesus says:

"Suffer little children, and forbid them not, to
come unto me; for of such is the kingdom of heaven."

Why are children this close to the Father?

These squalling, bediapered tyrants of the car-
riage and the crib, self-centered, screeching their de-
mands and turning purple-faced with rage if their
slightest need is neglected?

This four-year-old wrecking crew, hammer in one
hand and atom-ray gun in the other, bent upon unin-
hibited havoc?

The seven-year-old beribboned sweetheart who
runs to Mummy with stories of how the boy next door
pulled her hair, the girl upstairs stole her comic book,

the woman across the street slapped her face—none of which, it develops, is true?

To the average adult who is honest, little children are wonderful and exciting and—in varying degrees—creatures of unpredictable savagery.

What did Jesus mean, then, not in sentimental generalities, but precisely and expressly—by His repeated declaration "of such is the kingdom of heaven"?

Child of God—what is that?

Certainly it is the wisdom of innocence itself, the unknowing of evil.

Certainly it is the clinging fingers of discovery and delight, the child unfettered and unafraid.

Certainly it is the trust and love that the child—the average, normal child—gives to the life around him, to parents, environment, home, to his world as he knows it.

He bawls and screams and kicks, and this does not change the fact that he confidently expects an answer to his need. He is hungry and there is food. He is cold and there is warmth. The newborn infant knows this, instinctively and certainly.

The basis of this instinctive trust of the infant may be explained by psychology or by sociologists in varying ways, from prenatal consciousness to race memory, from evolutionary reflex action to primitive animalistic adjustment to environmental influence. A famous obstetrician holds each child he brings into the world into his arms and informs the newborn infant, "Everyone here loves you. Welcome to the world!"

Explains this doctor: "Some might not understand this. But the infant knows."

The child understands, accepts, expects.

Is not the faith of the child often disappointed? Are not children born crippled and blind and deaf and dumb? Do they not suffer loss and pain? Is it not true that the child must wake up to reality? Do we not use the phrase "growing up" to mean a coming to grip with reality on its own terms, rather than the fairy-tale terms of childhood?

We cannot avoid or evade this question, for it strikes to the heart of faith.

Yes, there are disappointments that the child en-counters; his expectation is often footless, his faith built on nothingness, his trust betrayed. That such things happen cannot be overlooked; that they present a philosophical and a religious problem of proportions sometimes almost unsurmountable cannot be denied.

This, however, is another question, entirely differ-ent from the meaning of the words of Jesus. He was using a symbolism: the faith of the child in relation to the parent; the faith of the adult man or woman in re-lation to God.

The beginning of faith is the beginning of our groping toward understanding—without assuming in advance that we know the answer. It is a hard fact, perhaps the hardest in all religion. Yet we cannot go ahead until we are willing to accept this point: We do not know everything, we have not advanced to the point where all answers are available to us.

A case in point is that of a child sick with a tumor of the brain. The doctors had given up all hope; it was merely a matter of time. This was a lovely little girl—one could indeed ask, "Why her? Why bring into the world a lovely little child like this, only to destroy her, in agony? Why bring her a glimpse of the beautiful things of life, only to tear them away? Why bring these parents their needless bundle of grief and despair?"

They prayed for this child, they asked the help of ministers to augment the work of the physicians. Day after day the child grew worse. And in the darkest moment of one difficult day, the eight-year-old girl in her bed said, "Don't cry, Mommie. God will take care of me."

But she died, this little eight-year-old.

Did faith die, too? Did God die, too, when this child in pain breathed her last on earth? Did these parents turn from God?

The answer is that the parents grieved, yet they clung to their faith. It was hard, gruelling, a struggle with the deepest emotions of which humans are capable.

It is not easy to discuss such a defeat as this. It cannot be explained away; it must be faced head on.

A little girl died? Why?

We do not know.

We do not know why many little girls have died, not merely this one. Little girls by the hundreds and the thousands, whose parents also prayed. And boys and young men and older people. The dead are strewn across the battlefields of a thousand wars and we do not know why—the dead for whom millions upon millions of parents and wives and sweethearts wept and weep.

Children and fathers and brothers have died in a hundred ways; trouble, catastrophe comes, striking out of nowhere. Defeat pours upon us. And mankind through the ages has wrestled with the question: Whom do we blame?

There are answers possible. One group will say that it was not God's will that this child should live. Another argues that it was His will, but that somehow the healing power was not reached. Others will say that no such divine power really works; when the body is infected too badly, nothing can be done. Another calls it Satan, the Devil, evil incarnate.

Beyond words is the simple truth of all faith: We are mortal; we are not God, and there are things we do not know and may not know for centuries or longer. Electricity was in the atmosphere; radio was possible, color television was possible a century past, or ten centuries; jet planes and atom bombs and man-made satellites were possible, had we but known.

How far we have come in such a handful of centuries, such a brief second in time, in our knowledge of the merely material things around us!

How much more, how vast an area of ignorance have we still to overcome, still to unfold in terms of the spiritual universe?

Faith is not in what we know, but in what we do not know and yet believe.

Our trust is in the intuitive certainty that God's will for us is good, that if we fail it is our failure, not His.

It is in the awareness that we are not God and cannot hope to be God.

And yet we must at the same time strive for certainty, for understanding, for victory, for perfection.

It is the goal, and the striving toward it, that is significant.

"Be ye therefore perfect, even as your Father which is in Heaven is perfect," Jesus tells us.

It is at once a remote goal for which we strive and an achievement available to any of us if we can learn to reach beyond our limitations.

"Don't cry, Mommie. God will take care of me."

The pattern is as wide as infinity, as elusive as wind and cloud and mist; the storm batters fields and forests and cleanses the air and brings drink to the roots and the seed; the patterns unfold; good emerges and evil feeds upon it and destroys, only to be turned into something else itself, as the forces we do not understand even make use of evil to bring good again.

We cannot play at being God or knowing all things, good and evil, nor does it make sense to turn from His strength in our failure. We can still seek to wrap ourselves in His love, in the perfect protection of His invulnerability.

To do this we must believe as a child believes, without question or reservation or secret motive, without anxiety or equivocation, without rancor or guile or guilt or perfidy, without hypocrisy or cant, without malice or ill will, without calumny or self-pride or self-hate, but with the full and overflowing force of love for God and His creation.

Is there yet an answer beyond our not knowing?

Lazarus was dead, and Jesus, his friend, wept before the tomb where Lazarus had lain dead four days.

And Jesus told Mary to have them move away the stone, and He lifted up His eyes and said, "Father, I thank thee that thou hast heard me.

"And I knew that thou hearest me always: but because of the people that stand by I said it, that they may believe that thou hast sent me.

"And when he thus had spoken he cried with a loud voice, Lazarus, come forth.

"And he that was dead came forth . . ."

Some who read may not believe in it, even now. They may doubt its authenticity. They may call it only an ancient story out of an olden book.

But others may recognize the covenant, the power that one day we may learn to use more fully, the spiritual force of perfect love and perfect faith and perfect concord, an invincible force that conquers even our implacable antagonist, death itself.

It is a promise for tomorrow, a candle for our night.

7

EPISODE

In the distance is our mountain, almost a dream. One does not see the road or the twistings, the cliffs or spurs or séracs or icefalls.

Far off it remains; but the past is here, the clutching memory that will not let go, the resentment, hurt and pain and defeat, the triumph of our enemy—all of it clings to us like an invisible encircling vine.

Too often faith is ruptured and destroyed for us, and the way is lost, in a single episode or moment of terror or despair that lives on in the shadows of our minds—and our souls.

A boy lies in a darkened room at an oceanside summer resort, but is not asleep. In the distance he hears the sound of surf, a resonant roar, crashing and dying away with a long withdrawing whisper.

In the next room a light burns. The boy can hear the voices of his parents. Familiar voices and words to which he at first pays no attention.

§ 72 §

Then he hears something unreal; it is out of a movie or television play, with people saying words that seem real but are not.

This is his father speaking: "How can I help it? These things happen, that's all. They just happen and no one can do anything about them. I meet someone else and fall in love with her. I can do nothing to change that; it is simply a fact."

The child listens. He tells himself it is a dream, the way things like this always are. He will awaken and there will be darkness and quiet.

"You want a divorce so you will be free?"

"That's right."

"To marry this woman?"

"Yes."

"I won't give it to you."

"But that would be foolish. Why make things more difficult? It only prolongs and drags out and hurts everyone."

"I won't give you one, anyway."

His mother is crying.

"You will have to, don't you see?"

It is not a dream. The child knows this now. It will not vanish in a moment or two; it is happening. All the reality of his brief experience suddenly is crashing around him.

His mother is saying, "You would force me—by any means possible—to give you this divorce?"

"If there is nothing else I can do."

"So I must surrender to a woman who comes in and smashes my home and family? I must give you to her?"

"We haven't been happy for years."

"I have."

"You haven't really. Neither have I."

"Our son thinks we're happy."

"We've put on a performance for him, that's all. It's wrong to live a sham, for any reason."

"For our son's sake, even?"

"It's too late, that's all. He'll be better off afterward. I know what's best."

"To run out on him?"

"Who's running out?"

"You're giving him up."

"Oh, no, I'm not. Oh, don't think I'm giving him up."

There is anger in his voice. The boy has heard this contemptuous tone before, when his father argued with a tradesman or a waiter, but not with his mother.

There have been quarrels before, and anger before, but the storms have broken and ended. All married people quarreled some of the time, his mother said once. It was part of nature, of life; people had to let off steam sometimes.

There had been quarrels and arguments and they had always ended with smiles and forgiveness, the child believed.

"I'll fight you all the way on this," his father is saying. "I'm not giving up my son forever because of your vindictiveness."

"Courts make the rules about that, I understand. If I go into court——"

"A father has rights, too. Just remember that. The courts permit a father to see his child. You can't keep me from my child."

"Oh, yes, I can. And I may. . . ."

To how many thousands of us did it happen in this or some similar way? To how many thousands is it happening now, in one way or another, one set of words or another, one pattern of havoc and destruction or another?

A boy lies in the dark and listens as the universe crumples. An eight-year-old—of such is the Kingdom of Heaven. Only in this case and for these people— of such is the kingdom of divorce. And of wrecked homes.

It is easy to explain an episode, to justify it, excuse it, condone it, to say that we must live for ourselves first, that the effort to compose differences is too great, that it is hardly worth it, that vows are only formal ritual in any case.

It is easy to make a mockery of our lives and our values, with or without divorce or open rift in the family.

The psychiatrist may have to probe these shadows, to ferret out the half-hidden episode that still

clamps its pain upon our lives, often without our realizing, long after pain should have died.

We hold on to such forgotten episodes sometimes
like children with battered toys that have become
symbols, dolls without eyes, carts without wheels. The
child is indeed father of the man, and the childish
moment of fear, loss, pain, grief, rage or frustration is
the father of grown-up hate, prejudice, irrational reaction, allergy and disease.

Above all, those half-forgotten episodes are parents of disbelief, forebears of a personal nihilism that
may leave our lives purposeless and without direction.

Rejection, shame, resentment, frustration, fear—
sudden and violent—an episode we don't recall that
poisons our lives and our faith and makes us unsure of ourselves and our world.

The tired episode out of the shopworn past clings
to us and will not let us go.

And often we do not recognize this latent force
that submerges itself in our religious life as in our
psychological patterns.

The child is young and will get over it, we insist.

We have a right to live our lives. And on our own
terms. We owe nothing to the public, to society, to
codes, provided we do not break any seriously en-
forced laws.

We have a right to our prejudices, our hates and
our dishonesties, we say. And if we get away with
them we will become leaders and heroes.

EPISODE

Sometimes, unhappily, it almost appears to work out.

But the road to faith, in such cases, is blocked by an avalanche and a cascade of destruction that crushes all in its path.

And far off the mountain is lost in mist.

A boy crouches naked in a darkened doorway, in a Midwestern city.

Outside the vestibule in the bitter winter night, his pursuers shout—neighbors, older youths, police. Now they have tracked him down, this naked ten-year-old boy running through the night.

In Sunday school, they had told him to love his neighbor and they did not ask whether he was white or black.

One day in a bus, when a Negro woman came in, holding packages, the ten-year-old arose and offered her his seat. The boy's father, sitting beside him, cuffed the youngster and told him to sit down. "You stupid kid," the father told him. "You don't give your seat to a nigger. I've got a stupid son. . . ."

The boy couldn't understand. A gulf developed between him and his father. The boy began running away from home, hiding out in a movie house. Sometimes he mixed with older men who offered him "sticks" of marijuana.

The police would bring him home and the father would thrash him with a strap.

On this winter eve the police brought the boy back around seven o'clock. The mother told him, "Get a bath while I fix you some dinner."

When the father returned a few minutes later and heard the story, he went into the bathroom and began to beat the boy as he stood naked in the tub.

Screaming, the naked boy ran out of the apartment and down the stairs into the street.

Others run after him, shouting in excitement as he streaks up the street. It is a gay madcap nightmare.

They gain on him and he turns and runs into the building and hides in the vestibule, trembling and wordless, with the crowd closing in from the street.

A case history of how a road to faith is lost.

It happens a hundred times a day, in different ways. Usually it stays hidden and unguessed behind family doors. Not very often does it erupt as this did into flight, and chase, with the authorities finally probing into the facts and helping a father and son together to explore the meaning of loving one's neighbors and one's own children.

Because this case brought in social agencies, and psychiatrists and child-guidance experts, the boy was given a second chance to find his road to belief in his world and his God.

How often does it go the other way? How many of us have laid the strap of our own hate and resentment and fear and prejudice and failure across the backs of our own children? How many of us have inculcated hate and taught it as a virtue? Love thy neighbor—provided he is of your own race, creed and color. And possibly of the same social station.

The path is lost for ourselves if we believe such things; it may be lost for others if we teach such things. The brotherhood of man must be the brotherhood of all men or it is a lie.

The child begins with his faith, absolute and unqualified. It is we—chance, society, prejudice, the shifting patterns of civilization, the fragility of purpose—all these tear away the inner certainty of the child. Too often faith is crushed before there is time for maturing conscious awareness.

The unborn faith is ripped out in many instances by adult words and dishonesties and shams, by lies and patent corruptions which the child sees through and either learns to accept or despise.

In some homes, we find the parent putting blame or abuse upon a child, for the parent's own guilt, his own failing, his own lack of faith.

Can a child be served up the teachings of hate, of duplicity and double standards in social and business customs, filled with ideas that wipe out decency and the whole validity of religious teaching—and still believe in the validity and importance and truth of those teachings?

In our moment of meditation, we know. The child who finds his father in a lie becomes a liar. If he catches his mother in deceit he becomes the deceiver;

when he finds hypocrisy in his parents, he becomes the hypocrite.

Or else, in rebellion against what he recognizes, he seeks to overturn all ideals and all belief.

How often and in how many ways do we hear the well-accepted adults spouting their hate to the young?

Or did it happen to us also?

For it may have happened in ways that no one guessed or knew about; even we may not have known. Rejection is so hard to accept that we seek excuses to believe it never happened. It may come in disguises, without open words or acts.

The product is the same. One child played against another, a parent or step-parent pretending love where there is no love; a word or phrase dropped in an unguarded second, "Oh, tootsie, why weren't you a little girl instead of a dirty-faced boy? . . . Now don't get that funny look. . . ."

Words that half say what they mean. Words that skip around like taunting dancers. "Stay outside, your father and I are talking business. . . ." How long will you wait beyond this door that closed, beyond laughter and love?

"Get out, Joey. Get out on the street and get yourself a job. You're a sixteen-year-old bum. . . ."

"What makes you think you're so pretty? You think you'll be a TV star? Honey, listen. . . ."

EPISODE

"You've been trouble from the day you were born. . . ."

In how many ways, to how many of us, did it happen?

Dr. Smiley Blanton, in his book Love or Perish, *tells us that we must begin by forgiving our parents for all the wrongs they did to us, real or imagined.*

This he calls the beginning of living a happy and fruitful existence.

And such forgiveness, by beginning to clear away the debris of resentment that blocks our road, is also a beginning of the way to faith.

8

UPWARD SLOPE

In spring the winds blow warm and cool.

In spring, all things are variable and shifting and uncertain in our lives.

We want to believe and sometimes we are afraid to believe; we want reality and we are afraid of reality; we want our dream and we are afraid of our dream.

We think of religion as a turning from reality; the adolescent glow believes that only the reality we can see and touch and taste is real; all else is fantasy.

We do not see that all things are spiritual, all things are the manifestation of God, all reality is good and all reality is one reality, of which we are forever a part.

In emerging youth—in the adolescence of years or of the spirit—there is danger that we can lose our way on treacherous, deceptive side streets that lead us on to nowhere.

§ 82 §

In the miasmic mist of adolescence, the patterns of faith are interweaving and befogged and lost in the distance. With awakening desires, hopes, fears, needs, uncertainties and doubts, there are torturing contradictions in purposes and desires. The adolescent would stand still and he would run; he would embrace and he would reject. He is man and boy, child and adult, mature and immature, positive at once that a thing is both true and false, beautiful and hideous, evil and good; he is certain that he can achieve whatever his dreams demand, and equally sure he cannot. He is in the world and of it, noisily and rambunctiously and with all his being; yet he is remote from it, apart and searching with his new, dream-ridden eyes.

The adolescent stands alone. Perhaps we stand near him, with our interest, our care, our love. Perhaps he will take all that we have taught him, or tried to teach him, about a road to faith and its twistings and its goals. Perhaps he accepts the past as his heritage, the familiar paths of ancestral creeds.

Ultimately, we know, he must make his decision, his choice; he must find his faith within his own mind and being. We may suggest and talk and direct and even plead; we may indoctrinate and preach; we may send him to this church school or that, this religious center of training or that; we may expose him to whatever truth we believe we have found.

However secure the adolescent may appear on

the surface, however completely he appears to accept the teachings of elders, the fact cannot be escaped that the verdict regarding the road he pursues—or does not pursue—is in his hands, his mind, his heart.

He sees a bewildering series of contradictions and confusions.

He sees a world that does not always add up to sense—but which adults tell him makes a lot of sense if only he would understand. He sees—when the mist momentarily lifts—roads crossing and recrossing, meanings crossing and recrossing. He glimpses a promise on the far mountain, beyond the hills, a green world of peace.

For an instant the vision emerges. To each young mind it is different; a new promise of Eden for the world or a new assurance of the kindly interest of the universe itself. Beyond the nearer ground—the nearer pain and hate and poverty and dishonesty and lies and deceit and all the rest he may have encountered or read or heard of—beyond immediate violence and the awakening needs of mind and body, beyond all of this, breaking through the haze and fog that sweeps his view, the green promise remains an instant, and is gone.

The promise—and the challenge—of the mist. Which road leads beyond the hills? And which turns off into disaster and defeat? Which is the path to understanding of this unpredictable life in which he finds himself? Who scales heights of glory in the brave new world of tomorrow's faith?

The shape of that faith—or of that tomorrow—is not yet clearly outlined in the mind of a boy or a girl with a bright dream and a willingness to charge forth into uncertainties, whatever they might be and wherever they might lead.

He seeks the right road and it must be a road to faith in his own terms; a road, if he examines it closely in his mind, that embraces the concept of love as a force or power or being.

But he does not always know.

How many times, if asked, "The right road to where?" his answer would have to be a wordless, adolescent shaking of the head.

A popular young singer has exaggerated sideburns; some of his fans follow suit, particularly in the adolescent age group.

Out of some weird pattern of thought, some adults equate the singer and the sideburns with youths who get into trouble. It is an equation that makes no sense and fits no reality. A reporter examines a thousand cases of deliquency, and finds the patterns of the backgrounds depressingly similar—the root causes are so standardized that any social worker or minister or priest who works with boys can tick the reasons off on his fingers. None of those causes include sideburns or singing—of any kind.

Yet listen to some learned judge in solemn robes, prescribing a haircut as a cure for a lad who gets into trouble.

Is right and wrong to be snipped off with a few locks of hair? Or is it merely a demand for conformity with the accepted fashions of the age and geographic location? Are sideburns of today a symbol of depravity—while those of great-grandfather's day were respectable and acceptable in good society? Do we still imagine that the world is going to hell because of the Charleston and the Black Bottom, dances which brought down denunciation over wide areas in the 1920's?

The adolescent who hears such arguments wonders how right and wrong are involved. It is in such foolishness that he becomes confused. A signpost in the mist emerges for an instant: "All without sideburns straight ahead. Others turn back here."

He wears sideburns because he wants to be thought of as a romantic—as youth has always wanted. Because he is in love with life and wants to savor its taste. He wears blue dungarees, because they are a uniform of adventure. He asks: Why are they wrong? Are the dungarees of themselves evil? To me, he insists, they are only excitement. One minute he is a cowboy and the next a sheriff or a stranger come to town. And the next he is only living, prowling the streets or the woods, the country roads, sitting on the hill gazing at the far-off mountain.

His questions require answers, not evasions. For what is most significant, in this adolescent era, is the increased awareness of life itself, of the world, of beauty, excitement—all reaching to the most remote star, and none of it unconquerable, all of it possible and within his reach. Where does he turn next? To dance wildly to a guitar, to lunge across a playing field, to hunt and fish and fight and shout and kiss and embrace and hold young softness in his arms? Is the awakening wrong? Is springtime evil?

"My beloved spake, and said unto me, Rise up, my love, my fair one, and come away.

"For, lo, the winter is past, the rain is over and gone;

"The flowers appear on the earth; the time of the singing of birds is come, and the voice of the turtle is heard in our land. . . ."

One cannot be frightened or ashamed or tormented by the wonders and beauties of the universe in which the Lord has placed us. That there are rules and principles under which we live—codes of morals, decency and behavior—is a fundamental fact. Promiscuity, licentiousness and absorption with the sensual are destructive.

But the soft green of the distant mountain is also a promise. Love, friendship, beauty, charm, music and laughter—even hot dogs cooked over an open flame—may also be products of Divine benevolence.

It is a splendid prize, the world of spring. The

mists clear and the sun shines and the road is wide and inviting. All the questions must be faced and all the answers must be explored and the laughter understood and the overflowing tears allowed. This is the wonder-time, exploring-time, the question-time, the awareness-time.

Accept it, understand it, channel it to the beautiful and clean and honest.

This, in essence, is the teaching of the great faiths of the world.

"The senses are great and powerful," declares the Bhagavad-Gita of the Hindus. "But greater and more powerful than the Senses is the Mind; and greater than the Mind is the Will; and greater than the Will is the Real Self.

"So, thus, recognizing the Real Self as higher than all, proceedeth thou to govern the Personal Self, by the power of the Real Self. . . ."

The road turns upward, the long sweeping gentle slope unfolds.

The world of beauty has its meanings and rewards to each individual who pursues his way. This world is dawning awareness of a God-oriented universe; without such glimmering intuition the path to faith would be lost in the mists for all our lives.

"There is, in sanest hours," Walt Whitman declared, "a consciousness, a thought that rises, independent, lifted out of all else, calm like the stars, shining eternal. This is the thought of identity—yours for you, whoever you are, as mine for me. Miracle of miracles, beyond statement, most spiritual and vaguest of earth's dreams, yet hardest basic fact, and only entrance to all facts. In such devout hours, in the midst of all the significant wonders of heaven and earth, (significant only because of the me in the center,) creeds, conventions, fall away and become of no account before this simple idea. Under the luminousness of real vision, it alone takes possession, takes value. Like the shadowy dwarf in the fable, once liberated and looked upon, it expands over the whole earth, and spreads to the roof of heaven."

The "Me" in all of this is Youth, the adolescent eyes, questing and hungry and wistful and in need, seeking a road across the world.

Faith in that youth—faith in the Self that God has given to us, the divine spark of awareness, faith in His creation—is faith in Him.

As we seek to recognize and serve the God-presence within ourselves and in others, so do we move closer to His way.

9

FOOTHILLS

The road at times is a narrow twisting trail.
Uncertainties become shadows and mirages;
one moment remote and elusive, the next close
and threatening.
We find ourselves afraid to deal with them,
afraid they will engulf and destroy us.
But truth cannot be obliterated for long by
mere shadows.

The guidebooks call them gentle, rolling hills.
No unattainable heights or sheer walls of rock loom
above us. Yet the beginnings of the highlands are up-
thrust and wooded, and begin to close in around us.

Sun splashes through in patterns of light and
shadow, in a shifting luminous magic—distant along
a ridge, transparent through the leaves of a line of
trees, a blaze of gold on the roadside where we stand,
or a hazy silver glow.

Abruptly, the road narrows. The trail is well
traveled, they tell us. It is well marked and not too

steep. You go forward, right over there. Leap the little gully. Work your way up through those few feet of bushes and undergrowth to the trail itself.

Now our road is only as wide as we are; we are in the thick of trees. Around us is the smell of the woods, a damp, sweet smell, a timeless odor of soft earth and young saplings and roots of trees that have withstood all onslaughts and still grow, and of fallen logs, green and moss-covered and dressed in fungus robes.

We are alone, yet not alone. There are climbers ahead of us and behind us on the trail; we are part of these people. Some stop by the side to rest; some are too weary, too fat, too worried, too conceited, to give themselves to any such ordeal as this. Others rush on, racing past us, joyful in the climb, caring for nothing except to reach the top.

We stay to the well-traveled path; it would be foolish to do otherwise. The hill has been climbed many times; all the questions have been answered a thousand times. What could we hope to gain by forgoing a path on our own, through the foothill forest?

The wiser ones keep to the trail. New worlds to conquer are not here but beyond; the heights are in the distance.

But this is a deep green world, this threading path that winds upward through the woods. We do not see the sun; foliage above and around us blots it out. There is warmth, density, an oppressive hemming in. The twigs of trees reach out at us, taunting us with uncertainties.

We do not talk much and in our silence our thoughts climb with us: What impulse is it that brings us to this trail, that drives us along this way, that pushes upward through these shadows?

The trail changes; we are at the top and no longer is the hill tugging at us. We stride forward easily. A few paces on we reach a break in the trees, a clearing with a view of countryside. We can see the stretch of woodland through which we have just climbed.

Before us are sun-splashed vignettes; scenes across the landscape, where the crisscrossing roads and lanes merge, widen, narrow, or roll on to the horizon.

We project our lives in vignettes such as these, ourselves, our experience, our albums of existence.

Our lives are shifting patterns, a kaleidoscopic series of episodes that impress themselves upon us; each leaves its mark, each is isolated, yet each is also a part of the others.

There are those we seek to recall and those we strive to rub out; there are memories that make or destroy us, buried memories lurking in dark corners of our souls; warm and wonderful memories which we cherish.

Each of these becomes a part of our faith, each

adds a little or takes a little away from the fabric of our being, out of which faith is molded.

Trivialities and meaningless moments become important, not in themselves but for this reason— that they leave their traces in a thousand invisible ways, in images we cannot erase:

The form of a man sprawled in the dark rain-washed night on the banks of the Seine. In my bad French I ask what happened.

The gendarme shrugs: *"C'est un homme mort, M'sieur. . . ."*

The late afternoon sun spilling on a crucifix in a church. . . . A woman who prayed in a foxhole in the Philippines, before a little shrine to the Virgin, murmuring special prayers in the bomb-ridden dark.

A madman's words . . . a child born . . . a frightened woman who knows she will die. . . .

A hundred scenes, a hundred moments, are there in the morning sun.

Here, a struggle in a doorway. This I wrote about as a reporter long ago because it happened and no one seemed to care.

Two men are fighting and one falls—blood runs on the street and the other man stands, tall and thin and full of terror, blood on his hands. The one who killed was recently out of prison, but the fight, people say, was not his fault. The other man attacked. But they are leading him off, sending him back to jail for all his life and you can hear him crying out, "It wasn't my fault, don't you understand? I didn't want to hurt him. He attacked me in that doorway. . . ."

Here is a family, father and mother and son. Hoodlums on the street have been attacking the boy and the father is saying, "Hit 'em back, son. Hit one of 'em, the biggest one. Hit one and the others will run."

The mother tells the boy to practice loving his enemies and returning good for evil. He must try to make friends with them, to turn the other cheek, to make himself a part of the group.

Later we hear the boy sob in the darkness. He cries out to his parents, "I tried it. I tried to be their friend. And it didn't work. . . ."

The father and mother argue and each blames the other, each insisting that a certain way is right; the mother tells the boy never to give up trying to love his enemies, and his father is shouting to punch them in the face. . . .

Here is a girl being married, warm and sweet in all her beauty. Her bridegroom wears a handsome rented suit and all the countryside gathers in the church, while the minister intones words ". . . whom God hath joined together let no man put asunder."

Music plays as the bride and bridegroom march out, arm in arm, and everyone shouts to them to go in this direction or that, their happiness lies this way or that. All are shouting at once and the bride and bridegroom are laughing. . . .

Look at this woman who thinks her husband is deceiving her when he goes out to play poker or have a few drinks with the boys. Ugliness steals over her face. The man recoils and turns away. She is driving him from her and pursuing him at the same moment. In their madness they writhe and twist from each other.

The moments crowd upon our thoughts with their foolishness and their insistence that we follow one road or another for reasons that make no sense. A politician shouts that we must be practical; deceit is permissible because everyone does it. Put your faith in making sure every voter believes in you; once you win do what you damn well feel like.

Others crowd in. Out of our past, our memory, our ancient hurt. Here is a funeral in a large cathedral.

Some great man has died and many are here to tell him good-bye—relatives and friends and enemies, even those who did not know him at all.

The cathedral is filled with these people; the bell tolls, and the service is chanted, the solemn mass; mourners kneel and stand and sit and kneel and stand again; the pallbearers carry the coffin out upon their shoulders and only a few close friends and relatives who say they loved him follow the cortege.

We hear a thousand voices from our vantage point, and witness a thousand dramas.

There is a family at dinner, mother and father, grown son and daughter. Behind them, on the wall above the dining-room sideboard, is da Vinci's painting of "The Last Supper" in a gilt frame.

It is not a very good reproduction. It lacks the pale iridescence of the original in Milan, the unearthly quality of the painting, which seems to have developed over the centuries, as if pigmentation and plaster and design and form and color have been transmuted into something beyond even the genius of the painter, into pure spiritual substance.

This family has never seen the original and does not think about the picture. Its force touches each of their lives, but they do not think of it consciously. They are laughing and talking about themselves; the boy is saying that he will be a jet pilot and the girl wants to be an actress on TV. And the parents shake their heads. . . .

An argument over here—the vestrymen and the school board are tearing at each other like children because a teacher named Scopes insists on telling his classes about evolution. This is criminal, the vestrymen say, and must be halted. What will our children believe if we permit such things? Evolution could not be taught, even if it were true.

Others are shouting that we must go through all schoolbooks and be careful what we say about everything and anything, be careful of fragile minds and above all don't put too much emphasis on this business of freedom of religion or freedom of belief or freedom of education because that kind of talk is dangerous. The road *they* want must have high walls.

A man cries out that it is only folklore, all of it, Noah and the Ark and the Flood and the Fall of Man. Here is another insisting that it is true, every word of it—the crafty Jacob who stole the birthright of his brother Esau, the Flood, the serpent in the Garden. *Literally* true. Not merely symbolically, but in actual fact. And anyone who disagrees is committing heresy.

The argument is real and alive around us. Do we or do we not accept all of this as literally true? Do we accept part? What do we accept and what do we reject? And what is the method of determination?

We catch other words and other groups: But, my dear fellow, there *are* witches and bewitched people and maybe it were well if some were hanged; it says in the Good Book itself that witches must be put to death. There are witches and heretics and ghosts that walk and Ouija boards that never fail to tell the truth and nothing but the truth. . . .

These are the words of learned men. They have spent long years of their life studying these things. They know all the theories and the answers, here and now in our own century.

They are arguing with other learned men. The

voices rise to a pitch of anger. We must believe them and them alone or we are lost.

The mirages and episodes vary; there is good and evil, blending and separating and merging again, interweaving shadows and images against the sun. . . .

There, on the deck of a destroyer in the Second World War—a man lies dead. He is a chief petty officer. His ship has made a hundred ports, a hundred actions in Pacific waters.

At every port of call he tried to purchase something for his children back home, some souvenir—a grass skirt, a model outrigger canoe, a drum, a war club, batik cloth from Samoa, a flower *lei* from Honolulu.

He would get them home, he wrote, in time for Christmas.

After the man was killed, his commanding officer sent the presents along to his wife in a small town in Texas. But when the sea bag arrived, and the widow opened it, none of the souvenirs from her husband were there. En route someone had gone through his effects and stolen all of the gifts he had collected.

The publisher of the Fort Worth *Star Telegram*, Eamon Carter, heard of this epilogue to tragedy and wrote to Admiral Nimitz about it. The time was short, he said; it was almost Christmas. The children of this man who had given his life for his country were expecting these few gifts as the last presents from their dad. Could not something be done in time?

§ 98 §

On Nimitz fell the entire responsibility for all naval and military operations over millions of square miles. But he managed to take a few minutes out to write an order to the admiral in charge of Fleet Recreation. Planes attached to Fleet Recreation—assigned usually to routine morale-building tasks—were ordered flown to every port in the Pacific at which the destroyer had called, to carry out Nimitz's command.

A full list of all the gifts the chief petty officer had purchased for his family was compiled. Officers and men were turned loose to scour these island-bases and obtain replacements for every single item on the list—dolls, toy boats and native drums, and model outriggers with real hollowed-out bark hulls.

And in the midst of war a navy plane winged across an ocean and half a continent to a town in Texas with a cargo of souvenirs of the South Pacific —with Christmas love from a dead war hero.

The scenes and episodes and memories move in upon us. There are so many voices and they are all so sure of themselves; they all know the way and they all are pointing and crying out.

How can they be sure? How can each know he is right? How can they point in so many ways at once, and why must they try to force us into their patterns. Why must we go their particular way?

Look at the twisting paths of their own lives, the

hodgepodge patterns, the good and bad, happy and unhappy, righteous and wicked, interlaced and criss-crossing so that we can hardly tell one from another.

There is the urge to try every road to its desti-nation, to test its mettle and purpose and meaning.

This way. Over here. You can't stay there; you'll be destroyed. The boy is a killer; let him rot in jail. It says inasmuch as you have done it unto the least of these, you do it unto Him. But that does not include everything, you know. Not the whole world. Temper spirituality with common sense.

This is the road. At that turn there. Don't bother with that family that prays all the time; they're noth-ing but fanatics, I suspect. It's all primitive nonsense, the way they go at it.

A hundred voices all at once; interpretations and exhortations and warnings and insistings shout at us and cry at us and demand of us, and do not seem to realize that we cannot hear in all the noise and de-mands. We must find our own way through this maze, this sunlit countryside of well-mannered belief and respectable doubt and nicely dressed denial.

We move forward through these conflicting cries.

We can listen only to the voice within; for the voices around us confuse and mislead, ridicule and defeat and turn us away.

§ 100 §

Do we have the courage to go on through this turmoil?

The answer lies in us, in the depth of our desire to reach out to God, to know Him.

10

STORY

Every life is a story.
Every human struggle a drama.
Each story and each life illuminates—or deceives.

And the closest to God are not the dazzling, but more often the most obscure, the unheard of, the overlooked.

Around the fireplace in the rustic lodge we sit and talk, strangers meeting in a moment of repose, trading stories and adventures and high excitement and terror that becomes pleasurable to talk about, because it is past.

It is evening time and we have turned from the road. Here in the lodge we have rested and dined and washed away the dust and sweat.

Flames dance in the fireplace and the shadows and glints of light play on the walls. The night outside is remote. We do not have to worry about ourselves, our beliefs or problems or fears.

STORY

Outside the wind frets, and loneliness is real; we close the doors against it. We steal moments like this, steal them from the dark.

After we dine we tell our stories around the fire, and the others lean forward and smile and seem to listen, but no one listens really, or at best only a little.

We also listen a little and watch the flames, yellow and gold and blue, flickering and flaming in the hearth. There is hypnotic quality in flames; they cast a spell with their dancing.

Each of us tells his story, and each is different and each the same. The flame draws out each deeply hidden, carefully nourished memory.

The flame drags up memories and each tells his in his own way, as he wants to tell it, as he remembers it, or reshapes it, as he sips his brandy, or his coffee, and watches the firelight. Each is warm and safe in this place, warm and safe within himself, warm and safe for tonight. We do not know or think about tomorrow.

One does not ask of what the firelight is made, or how long the flame lives.

How long ago was it, this story you tell?

The others listen, and words spin out. You were still a child then, and you did not understand all the things that happened until later, until you pieced together the facts.

This was your grandfather and he was alone. You were too young to understand and the family was scattered.

He was short and stocky—everyone said he had a bad temper, but it didn't mean much really; he lost his temper and shouted, but he never meant to hurt.

He was always making mistakes. He would go into more business ventures and fail more often than almost anyone in the world and it was never his fault; it was always luck. A ticket agency would thrive —until the railroad closed up and the ticket office with it. An excelsior factory was a big success, but he could not get fire insurance on such a place and one day it burned down.

He would go broke and then he would be back again with something new and exciting in which he would put his faith and his talents and energies. He put his faith in God and in work and in never giving up.

On the occasion when he lost everything, he was sixty-five, veteran of many battles in the world of business, and he was alone, penniless and whipped.

That is what people said.

With him, it was different. He believed in the strength of God. Sometimes he would tell you that and you would not understand. How could God's strength work to help you?

One day you learned the way it worked with him.

§ 104 §

In the midst of his defeat, as these others saw it, he had walked one morning into the office of a large company dealing in optical goods.

The president of this firm had heard of the old man's plight and was kindly.

"I wish I could help you. At present, there's no opening that a man of your experience——"

"I can take on almost anything."

"There's nothing."

"I can sell. I've been selling for half a century."

Finally, the president relented a little. "There's one possible spot—in Maryland. Selling. We've a part-time man who's turned in only a couple of hundred dollars' worth of business in the past month. Maybe you could better that."

The old man said, "When do I leave?"

"Whenever you're ready. There's no hurry."

"I can make the eight-forty plane."

The other man looked startled. "You know the schedule?"

"I've been there before."

A few days later, orders began to come in from the new salesman in Maryland. They came in a flood. By the end of the first day of this flood, more than ten thousand dollars' worth of orders had arrived. The next day it was five thousand dollars more. And five thousand the day after that.

It was obvious that the old man had lost his mind, they decided. The firm did not do business on such a scale. "Pile them up on the desk," the company president instructed.

Just as they thought the storm had ended, telegrams and phone calls began to pour in from retail stores all over the state of Maryland. Where were the shipments? What happened to those barometers? And the cameras?

The firm that had imagined itself saddled with a half-demented salesman suddenly found itself in the greatest rush of its history, filling thousands of dollars' worth of orders piled unanswered on the desk.

Over the long-distance phone they were trying to explain to their new star salesman how the delays had occurred, apologizing for their doubts, telling him not to worry, shipments were starting; they would work through the night.

Within a year, he became vice-president in charge of the sales staff. From being alone and beaten, he had become the much-loved grand old man of that firm.

Once, I remember, I asked him what he had done in Maryland that was so different; how had he been able to sell so much where everyone else had failed?

"Sell?" he said. "I didn't sell anything. I just dropped in to see a few friends. Old friends. All over the country, over fifty years, I made friends like that. People in whom you could put your faith."

The winds whisper beyond the walls.

People in whom you could put your faith, he said. Friends in whom you could put your faith. The world in which you could put faith.

And people trusted him—and what he told them about his product—because they could rely on him as a man of faith.

The quality of faith itself has its meaning, and its force, and its strength. Go your way, Jesus tells us —your faith has made you whole.

But unfaith then is like the winds outside, whining and ripping and seeping in through unprotected cracks.

Here in the lodge we sit and talk and listen, and each tells his story, stories of others they have known who would not surrender. There is always someone in each of our lives to give the example of triumph.

The leaping flame dies down.

The deep red warmth of the coals pervades the lodge.

We may not understand the nature of good and evil, or the workings of the Almighty God.

But it would be difficult not to see His power and work, in the life of this man.

It is a power equally available to us in our need.

11

INTERLUDE

But to come to the heart of our own doubts and questions and uncertainties and ambivalences, we must be willing to explore not only matters of faith and the ultimate reality, but the immediate questions of the world around us.

If we seek truth on which to build our lives, there can be no areas or paths where we dare not look, no doors we dare not open, no facts or concepts we dare not consider.

If there is forbidden fruit, may we not, as children of the Father, seek to understand?

Where is there a corner of creation that we dare not gaze?

In the valley between the foothills and the mountain we reach the town, and beyond the town the university, the citadel of truth, the repository of integrity of mind.

It is curious how exactly town and university fit the picture shaped by time-tested tradition, the familiar picture, repeated ten thousand times in ten thousand other towns in ten thousand other valleys.

Here is the fortress of free thought, the outpost of the intellectual, where generalissimos of learning pour out their distilled findings, stripped of the sentimental, the wishful, the sticky-sweet.

Yet among these same craggy defenders of the unsentimental we find a most extraordinary sentimentalism—of which they sing and talk with nostalgic wonder—the campus and the elms, the ivy-covered lecture halls, the professors with their dreamy Mr. Chipsian expressions, clinging to their dogmas and theories and hypotheses, defending their corollaries and implications with fervor; to be forced to admit an error you do not discover yourself is even more catastrophic than to suffer defeat on the football field, which for years now has supported the entire institution and paid most of the salaries of these same professors.

Hiring athletes and calling them students is venal only in a controlled measure, and if it produces funds by which the professors are enabled to teach their students ideas and ethical principles, how can one attack it as morally wrong? Does not the end justify the means that enables them to teach that the end does not justify the means?

Thus the beautiful duplicity of the ivy-covered halls. It is a quaint, scholastic dishonesty, one which may cause a professor alone behind his desk to smile out of the window, a gentle duplicity that certainly cannot match in evil or intent the boundless evils of the outside world.

Besides, there are many kinds of minds and morals, are there not, and wouldn't it be wrong to practice only one kind of morality in a place of learning?

This is a place of preparation for what lies beyond. We are inclined to forget its importance, this world of schools and colleges and massive universities, this training ground of bodies and minds and souls. And because so much of what happens here, especially in regard to the students, is only rehearsal, it becomes terribly important and significant and must be discussed and debated and examined from every side. For here the students put aside, perhaps for the first time, the childish dream and begin to explore realities.

So many do not understand. So many outside of the university are afraid. So many cannot grasp the need and would prefer to see thought die on the stiffling parasitical vines of fruitless conformity.

We are inclined to forget, I think, how important it is that young people have this time, free and unfettered, to find the truth. Remember how the elders fretted over a generation that grew up in depression and turned to socialism and left-wingism? Everyone thought they would tear civilization down; instead they went out to war on our enemies and defeated them on battle fronts all over the world, to prove that freedom as we know it, imperfect as we may be, is worth living and dying for. Where did they learn this but in the matrix of freedom itself, in the examination of ideas from every side, at the point where freedom should walk with greatest pride—the high places of learning?

We forget how important is this young, contradictory, freedom-spun world of dormitories and gyms, lecture halls and tobacco shops, the "Co-op" and the night cafeteria where students drink coffee and debate subjects students have always debated. The townspeople live off the students and love them and hate them, embrace them and battle with them and accuse them; but "town and gown" have been that way for centuries.

This is the unpredictable world of the academic, of chalk and lead pencils and lecture notes and pious impieties, meaningful and ridiculous, practical and impractical, realistic and idealistic, pompous and humble, all at once.

This is the beginning of maturing faith, of faith that may deny itself, or that may stumble down some ancient path to long-forgotten realities.

The professor is small and bent and forgetful. Professors mirror the personalities they are supposed to have, exactly as do the ivy-covered halls and the elms and all the rest, the glee club on the steps of the library in the spring twilight, the quiet, cloistered atmosphere and the clutter of a student's room. His subject is geology and he is wise. Sometimes, looking down upon his students, he seems so old and they so young; he seems as old as time, as the rocks of which he talks and the fossils found in them, the striations of glaciers long since melted away, the tiny fragile skeletons of sea things long extinct, or the bones of the Brontosaurus and Tyrannosaurus.

"The dinosaur," he intones, "put on heavier and heavier armament to protect itself from its enemies, until at last it was the most heavily armed creature in all the world, but at the same time its brain grew smaller and smaller until finally the brain weighed only an eighth of an ounce, half in its head, and half at the base of its tail.

"And with so little gray matter he was no match for clever creatures like monkeys, for example, who could drop coconuts on his foolish head, or for the demands of the elements, and the environment, and so the dinosaur perished from this earth. . . ."

The professor knows well the hazards of the roads beyond the university and the valley; he insists that whatever road his students choose—the flat and secure path to success and summer homes, the high dangerous road of courage and dedication, or the perilously twisting, mirage-ridden but still beckoning trail to faith—whichever one they take, he insists, they must be fortified with knowledge and understanding.

"Learn, learn, learn," he cries. "Without learning all is lost, and the road that is sunlit in the morning is storm and death in the darkness. And you can be forced back and down and the avalanche buries you, unless you know. . . .

"Your equipment, your training, your reason, your depth of understanding—these are the tools for your journey. Take with you knowledge and integrity and willingness to face truth on its own high terms."

He looks around at the questioning young men and women in his class.

"How do we know what is truth, Professor?"

"You do not know it. But you can recognize it. But you may not admit the truth even to yourself."

"Why won't we?"

"I did not say you won't, only that you may not. It depends on how frightened you are, or how frightening the truth itself may be."

"So truth is frightening?"

The professor is annoyed at the student's persistence. "It depends on how you look upon it," he answers.

"What is faith, Professor?"

"A kind of knowledge, based on intuitive perception, in most instances, rather than factual data. The reasons may be sound or unsound, physical or metaphysical."

"What if it does not work? If you have faith in God and you ask some favor and it is not granted?"

"Well, we have a choice. You may give up your faith that there is a God Who answers prayers. Or you may decide that your request is denied; that you have asked amiss."

The young mind listens and questions and wonders.

The white-haired professors of science walk with eyebrows drawn in politely furrowed frowns, and the young instructors stride with confidence. Have they not reached into the sea of space with new rocket propulsions that will carry them who knows how far? Have they not turned, in the other direction, to the infinitude of the infinitesimal?

Listen, they say: Long years ago the faith of men of science in sanitation put an end to plagues that had destroyed whole populations, plagues that the world had called visitations of the devil of punishments. If these were punishments or visitations, how could such a mundane thing as good plumbing wipe them out?

The young mind listens and wonders and the professors and their associates pour out their endless waterfall of facts, and crushing torrent of footnotes, and footnotes to footnotes. Religion must forever war with Science, states the science professor, with unscientific certainty.

Listen: Ancient peoples designed the heavens and the gods to fit their own ideas and their own needs. The people of the sea had sea gods and the people of the mountains had mountain deities and the people of the forests worshiped trees and vines, and people of the blazing equatorial zones worshiped the sun.

What heretic dared to say that the world was not the center of the universe? Who believed this fellow Copernicus? Was not this old man Galileo forced to recant his heresy that the earth revolves on its axis? And what of the teacher in Tennessee who dared to say that men were descended from the Paleozoic ooze?

The man of science cites case after case in the long struggle of religion against the scientists; from theories of demons floating around in the air a few hundred feet off the ground, to books and treatises and learned factual reports on witchcraft, and all the foolishness and cruelties of clergymen who went through the countryside finding witches to put to death.

The professor quotes from a learned authority, Theodore White, in his work, *The Warfare of Science With Theology:*

"Still the geologists continued to seek truth: the germs planted especially by William Smith, 'the Father of English Geology,' were developed by a noble succession of investigators, and the victory was sure. Meanwhile those theologians who felt that denunciation of science as 'godless' could accomplish little, laboured upon schemes for reconciling geology with

Genesis. Some of these show amazing ingenuity, but an eminent religious authority, going over them with great thoroughness, has well characterized them as 'daring and fanciful.' Such attempts have been variously classified, but the fact regarding them all is that each mixes up more or less of science with more or less of Scripture, and produces a result more or less absurd."

Men of philosophy pose other questions: Is God really God or only a projection of the Freudian father-image? Or is He a national or racial Ego or Super-Ego or Id? Or is it possible, as Jung insists, a fact of the universe that the intuition of God remains the strongest and deepest of our drives?

These are answers you must work out for yourself, the professor declares. Reasoned heresy is better than unreasoned orthodoxy. What about Kant and the categorical imperative? Can our ideas on religion stand up under the microscope? What is your idea about guilt and original sin? Are you guilty? If so, of what? Or is your guilt merely weakness or fright or despair?

And if we are going to be rational about it all, what kind of facts do we demand for proof?

"It is particularly in religion that the objective truth is the only thing that can set us free," Harvard's Professor Hocking once wrote in his study of pragmatism. "For religion is the orientation of the human self to what it regards as the most real thing in the world. God is nothing if not that on which we depend. But every chosen belief, every manmade idea of God . . . palpably depends on us. . . . If we can get no evidence in religious matters, we must go without it; for here most of all the possibility of a negative answer to our hopes must be kept open. . . ."

But what is objective truth? The devil's sending plagues—or the new sewer pipe carrying away the slime out of which the plague is really produced? Does the objective truth lie in our urge to God, in the impulse that leads to religious faith, regardless of its detractors and of religion's admitted errors and even brutalities in many parts of the world?

Is there a world-soul to which the individual soul reaches out, as rain trickling down a pane of glass reaches for the sea?

Listen: The professor speaks of Zen, the reality that is not, the nonreality that is. "From the beginning," declares the professor, quoting Hui-Neng, "not a thing is." The Perfect Way envisions and allows no preference, the mind is neither for nor against anything at all, truth cannot be found in the search, neither like nor dislike, neither hate nor love; do not either oppose or accept, only allow your mind to dwell in vacancy, since there is no good or evil, no right or wrong, no light or shadow, but only the radiant beauty of the nothingness.

Such is Zen, the professor declares, and the student's mind echoes without preference and without rejection familiar words suddenly twisted into grotesque meaninglessness: "As it was not in the Beginning, is not and never shall be. . . ."

And he runs suddenly from the mystic mouthings. He has seen them, he has listened, he has looked. But consciousness sweeps through him, and awareness, and he knows that, if reality is a mirage, then mirages must exist; and if it is a mirage of a mirage, still that must be real; and it can go on endlessly like an infinity of reflections in a mirror, until it reaches the ultimate which all the great religions of the world agree is the only reality, however it may be manifest.

But when we speak with the professor in person he holds no brief for Zen and its spiritual nihilism, but quotes instead a few lines from Thomas a Kempis: "Nothing, therefore, is more sweet than love, nothing higher, nothing stronger, nothing more joyful, nothing fuller, nor anything better in heaven or in earth; for love descendeth from God, and may not rest finally in anything lower than God."

Here in this valley interlude, in these classrooms, guided by thoughtful unfrightened men, a strange storm rages, an invisible storm of possibilities. Nothing is too sacred here to be looked at with candor, to be subject to the most exhaustive analysis; no idea, no prejudice, no creed, no theory, no custom, or ritual, habit or holiday too untouchable to become a laboratory problem.

Do not be frightened of the storm, the professor remarks. It is part of the academic way, the violence of ideas, the clashing of concepts, the exposure of tawdriness and sham, past and present.

Throughout our lives there are the teachers, sometimes kind and gentle; sometimes harsh, cruel, even destructive; sometimes remote and Olympian.

The Professor of Literature is not a man of any church, but he is a man who understands beauty and form and meaning, and he quotes the great poets of truth. Listen to a stanza from Emily Dickinson, he advises. Listen to her words as he quotes:

> *"I never spoke with God,*
> *Nor visited in heaven;*
> *Yet certain am I of the spot*
> *As if the chart were given."*

He turns to others of whom we have heard, Emerson, Thoreau, Holmes and Whittier. And Walt Whitman:

> *"There was never any more inception than there*
>   *is now,*

Nor any more youth or age than there is now,
And will never be any more perfection than
*   there is now,*
Nor any more heaven or hell than there is now."

The professor is impartial; believe or not believe; it is not his concern. Believe in Greek mythology or Roman, in transendentalism, or in the Puritanical creeds of Increase Mather or Anne Bradstreet.

Chaucer or Rabelais or Milton, Aristotle, Longinus or Thucydides—the professor leaps from one mind to the next, one glory to another, like a museum guide.

But sometimes he lingers lovingly over a single phrase.

And here is a teacher, old and white-haired, tall and lean. A Professor of the Bible. It is said on best authority that no one in all the university or the valley or the world knows quite as much about the Scriptures and what they mean and from whence they came as he. The greatest scholars of the world beat their way to his cottage on the edge of town to talk with him, and students crowd into his classes because they say no other man can make these things come alive as he can; he acts out Bible scenes right on the platform.

His treatment of the Book of Ruth, they say, is

classic; he tells the story of Naomi and her daughter-in-law, Ruth, as if he were revealing personal details of his own relatives.

For Naomi's husband, Elimelech, died, and her two sons, Mahlon and Chilion, also died, and Naomi after the custom of that time told her daughters-in-law to go home to their people, to find new mates, new lives and new happiness. For I am old, Naomi tells them, and can produce no more sons to be your husbands. "Turn again, my daughters, go your way . . ."

Old and white, tall and lean, his lips drawn tight and his hands clasped behind his back, the professor strides up and down the platform and tells again the story, of the daughter-in-law, Orpah, who went home to her people, and of Ruth who would not go. And how Naomi declares, "Behold thy sister-in-law is gone back unto her people, and unto her gods; return thou after thy sister-in-law."

Some recall how the professor is always deeply moved as he relates all of this, explaining the story and its meaning, the sweep of this trivial incident out of history and legend, poetry and religion. It is one human being and another, two people torn by loss through the death of those they love, two who find strength in clinging to each other, to the same faith, to the same God. There is a cosmic loneliness and need, he says, in the cry of Ruth: "Entreat me not to leave thee, or to return from following after thee: for whither thou goest, I will go; and where thou lodgest, I will lodge: thy people shall be my people, and thy God my God. . . ."

The professor's voice breaks a little at these words, and the students gape at him in great emotional silence, and afterward talk about his "performance" and laugh, but few can deny they are deeply stirred, even those superior minds that discount the possibility of spiritual implications.

Now he comes to his last lecture before retirement to some corner of the valley with his books and notes—to rest, he comments, to dream and remember and die.

The lecture hall is thronged; there is no place even to stand; outside, students climb the ivy to the windows—to cling precariously and listen.

Today, as always, in the final lecture of the term, the professor talks about Ecclesiastes, or the Preacher. He discusses the possible sources of the work and the evidence for and against its attribution to Solomon.

He discusses the book's meaning, its pessimism, its sense of oppression and despair. All this he speaks of quietly, dispassionately; it is only one more lecture to his class.

When will he begin? his listeners wonder. This is all so prosaic. They say he can really put on an act. There is a stirring in the class.

He opens the Bible and begins to read, his voice sharp and dry as old voices often are:

"Vanity of vanities, saith the Preacher, vanity of vanities; all is vanity.

"What profit hath a man of all his labour which he taketh under the sun?

"One generation passeth away, and another generation cometh: but the earth abideth for ever. . . .

"I communed with mine own heart, saying, Lo, I am come to great estate, and have gotten more wisdom than all they that have been before me in Jerusalem: yea, my heart had great experience of wisdom and knowledge.

"And I gave my heart to know wisdom, and to know madness and folly: I perceived that this also is vexation of spirit.

"For in much wisdom is much grief: and he that increaseth knowledge increaseth sorrow."

He closes the book and holds it tightly in his hands. "Vanity of vanities," he repeats. "All is——"

He looks around at his class. "Gentlemen, those are the words of a *disappointed* teacher, of a man who had lost faith in himself and in his students. . . . Gentlemen, I thank you that I am not as that man."

Tears are in his eyes as he turns away.

Vanity of vanities, we think. All of it uselessness, meaningless, nothingless. All of what? All the knowledge they have piled up? All the great corridors of progress, all the tall buildings and superjet rockets and satellites and sataloids?

Vanity of vanities? We turn again to other verses in that same book of the Preacher:

"Remember now thy Creator in the days of thy youth, while the evil days come not, nor the years draw nigh, when thou shalt say, I have no pleasure in them;

"While the sun, or the light, or the moon, or the stars, be not darkened, nor the clouds return after the rain. . . ."

Such is the university and its challenge, its clash of words and ideas, its furnaces of white-hot truth and fact and falsehood, all to be examined and studied and decided upon.

Vanity of vanities?

The professor of science shakes his head in disagreement and turns back to his test-tube universe.

Such is the valley and its town. Beyond, the road twists into shadows.

There is no corner where you dare not look.
Do not be afraid for your faith; it must be
strong enough to withstand falsehood.

No idea, no concept, however, do we dare not
explore.

No philosophy—however daring or novel or

arrogant—so long as we understand it and its truth or falsity, can injure faith.

Seek to understand ideas in their completeness, in their truth or falsity.

Seek to understand reality in every aspect, in so far as you can.

Seek to explore the shadows and the sunlight equally, for both are of God.

12

VISTA

To learn to listen to the inner prompting is not easy, for the world is too much upon us, too much a part of our lives, too immediate, too insistent upon itself.

The whisper within says that we can know only a fragment of reality through the merely sensory perception, or the purely intellectual apparatus.

The finite roads become blind alleys walled in by voiceless night.

The true adventure of faith leads in another way.

We walk alone into the dawn, along a road beyond the valley and the village. It is dark and the houses are unlighted and we are young and unsure.

Loneliness sets in like oppressive fog. It is so in youth; it does not matter who or what we are, whether we live with well-meaning folks who may or may not understand, or alone in some rented room.

VISTA

Loneliness deepens like the quiet because it is within us, compounded of conflicts and uncertainties, desires and dreams; it becomes a magic thing, interesting but disturbing. What do we believe now, we wonder, now that we are adult and mature?

The university is behind us, and the campus town. We walk into the new and the undiscovered. It does not matter that it is old as time itself, as darkness itself, for it is new to us.

We have been climbing steadily since the valley, but the road is wide and the slope gentle. Behind us we can see a few scattered lights of early risers in the valley below.

There is dampness in the air, the cool damp of the dawn. As the sky brightens, moisture glistens on leaves and grass and hillside.

The sun is breaking through, behind the line of trees.

Today belongs to us.

And what is the village of the upper valley?

It lies ahead on our road. It lies ahead on all roads, perhaps, a composite of compromise and mediocrity, a sellout of the human soul for a measure of security and creature comfort.

We cannot understand the problem of achieving faith unless we understand the upper-valley village, and its people. We cannot look down at them, or criticize or condemn them. But to understand them and what they are we must at least look at them squarely and objectively.

The upper-valley village is pleasant in the morning. This is a well-run suburban community. It sits on the hillside, amid well-kept shrubbery and back yards and front yards and driveways and two-car garages. Its people are well prepared to defend what they believe from any onslaught from any quarter. What they believe is a mercurial matter that depends largely on whom you talk with, who else is present, how many drinks they have had, and the status of things as of closing time that afternoon.

They go to church on Sunday in upper-valley village. Almost everyone goes; not to go, unless you are terribly rich or terribly poor, is to be an outcast. Going to church is a social must.

They get drunk and gossip and quarrel and hate and envy; they are jealous and vengeful and small; they say the cruel thing and the bitter thing and the needless thing, and they go to church and they pray.

They may seduce a neighbor's wife, or cut his throat in a quick turnover; they may force him to the wall and compel him to lie or cheat only to stay alive, but they go to church because they must, because the minister or rabbi or priest insists.

Some of these men and women were undergraduates in the university long ago; on Saturdays after football games in the autumn there are always parties at some of the houses and the men become boys again for a few hours and relive past glories.

They fall into patterns in upper valley. They wear white shirts and proper ties and they say and do only the right thing and proper thing and they become emotional to the right degree and righteous to the proper extent and wrapped up in some cause or other within bounds.

Even so, despite whatever compromises they make, despite feuds and bickerings and internecine neighbors, they have another side as well: they search for the real, they reach out, they yearn for fulfillment.

Some have banded together, some of the best people and the business leaders, the professional people and the publisher of the weekly paper; they have agreed on their purpose—to put religion to work in the life of this town.

It has to be something more than just Sunday service, they all agree. "It's good to go to church," they point out, "but we can't stop there. We have to make our religion work and we do that by putting it into practice not just once a week, but every day of our lives."

They say such things, and mean them deeply.

And so they go into activities for community funds and fighting deliquency and improving the chance of young people to get together for Saturday-night dances on a proper basis; they fight crime and corruption and disease and poverty and they raise funds for the new church—and everyone gives something regardless of faith.

And on Sundays they go to church and kneel and pray.

It is an average upper-valley town, no better or worse, with people no better or worse, than ten thousand others like it, across ten thousand years of towns.

This is the main street with its stores and post office and hairdresser and movie house and bank and church. Running off to the side are narrow streets that lead into tree-shaded residential areas. And people are forever saying that the town isn't the way it was, and how it has changed, with new people coming in, and you would never know the place.

Elm Street crosses Main; to the left it goes over the railroad; that isn't too good a district. The better homes, the nicer ones, are off to the right. Here are the larger, newer places, big lawns and shade trees and well-kept shrubs and terraces and garages, and in late autumn the smell of burning leaves fills the air.

Elm Street to the right is wide and runs into narrow twisting Country Club Road, which leads on up the hill to the club. Beyond that is Shrub Oak Hollow, the most exclusive residential part of town, where really important people live, those with real money and power.

VISTA

The streets are few and their names familiar. Elm and Pine and Main and Maple. You find yourself wandering from one to the next; you feel trapped, they are all so alike, streets and pavements and mailboxes and driveways and houses; it is a labyrinth of sameness.

At the corner we find a turning, and the road tips over a hill. There are houses here also, not so modern or stylish, and along this street we find ourselves in a different kind of district. The houses are small and ramshackle, weather-beaten and sagging; there is an auto repair shop and a junk yard. The street is dirty and unpaved, the doorways lead into dark entrance halls and rickety stairways. Dogs scrounge in the gutters, but you see no people.

You walk unpaved streets and now you know that you are truly alone; you are not a part of this street and do not understand it. You walk past crumbling, dilapidated houses, a grocery store with boarded-up windows, an unpainted church with unpainted steeple sticking into the sky, past the junk yard with its piles of worn-out auto tires and broken chairs and fragments out of people's lives.

A child runs from a doorway, a golden-haired, blue-eyed girl who stumbles and falls—we hurry to help her up and she is not weeping but laughing; her laughter ripples across the sunlit morning as she turns and runs.

THE ROAD TO FAITH

The child's laughter echoes in our thoughts.

The road is suddenly narrow, it is no road at all, hardly a trail, sharply rising before us. We drag and push and claw our way through an undergrowth of bushes and weeds that crowd in around us, a suffocating, strangling barricade.

We scratch against the sides of rock and pull ourselves free.

It is only a brief thing, this contretemps at the edge of town. The labyrinth is behind us, and the backwash of despair.

Only the echo of the child's laughter, like an unfinished promise, remains.

The path widens. Around us is the sweet smell of a pine grove. We hurry forward, through the shifting lights and shadows of the trees.

Here on the edge of the grove we lift our eyes to the distant mountain, to its high sheer cliffs above the deep greens and golds of the forests. We do not know by what route we will reach above those cliffs, to the gray-gold spur of rock that curves upward to the high peak.

Who goes with us now, who scales these heights that loom before us?

We go alone.

Alone, or with strangers, silent associates, thousands upon thousands, strangers and brothers.

VISTA

We travel together, we share together, yet we go alone.

The height must be reached by each of us in this aloneness, accompanied only by the God we seek.

13

VISION

As we learn to listen to the inner prompting, so we learn also to see with the inner eye.

The eye of the soul illuminates the whole being, for it sees all things in truth.

But the understanding of self, and the seeing of self, is an essential step on the pathways of faith.

Otherwise, we cannot know who we are really, or our true relationship to all the universe.

The ear must hear, and the eye must see, and the mind must understand, for each is an integral part of faith.

We have gone a little way. But from the place we have reached, we have seen the stupendous way we still must go to achieve this summit.

We cannot plunge blindly forward without thought or experience or consideration, hoping to stumble on the proper road.

We can hope to make this ascent through self-knowledge, in its deepest meaning. We must know our own reservations, our willingness or unwillingness to face truth as our understanding permits, our willingness to explore, to examine, to risk.

Only in such self-probing can we prepare ourselves for the high conquest before us.

To some, faith comes as a grace and we do not know how or why. This is not merely a theological theory; it is empirical in the sense that there are those who have faith and those who—brought up in the same environment and under almost exact conditions —cannot believe even when they wish to believe.

Religious and inspirational writer, Mabel Thurston, tells in one story of a boy who had a blind father to whom he was deeply attached. The father and son were inseparable comrades until it came time for the boy to go to college.

"The separation was terrible for both of them," she writes, "but the boy went, determined to make a record for his father's sake. He did make a record, both in his work and in athletics where, presently, he made the football team and became its star player. The college was looking forward to his leading the team to victory against a formidable rival when he received a telegram telling of his father's sudden death. The whole college went into mourning. Their hope of victory vanished with their star player out.

"The boy came back from the funeral the day before the game. Nobody dreamed that he would play, but to their amazement he presented himself as usual. Not only that, but he played as no one had ever seen him play before, and led his team to a glorious victory."

After the game, this writer relates, the team captain came up to the boy and tried to tell him how grateful everyone was. "We didn't think you would want to play," the captain stated.

"But you don't understand," the boy said quickly. "Don't you realize—*this was the first time my father ever saw me play.*"

This youth had no need to scale any mountainside. He had attained his goal long ago, and only a fool or idiot would seek to destroy or injure or tear down that kind of security.

Most of us, whatever we may say on the surface, whatever we may pretend to accept, have deep within us certain reservations and doubts. Even when we think we believe, we may doubt and question and even deny.

How many times do we find ourselves perched on this perilous ledge, halfway between faith and doubt, and not certain which way we think we want to go? Not sure, either, that if we try to achieve faith, we may not destroy the honesty and integrity of ourselves.

"Nearly everyone," Miss Thurston writes, "has faith in some kind of a God. Nobody is worrying very much, for instance, for fear that the earth will collide with any other planet. We have faith in a God Whose laws work unfailingly in the physical universe. But that is a very different thing from having faith in a God Who cares if anyone is hungry or unhappy or sick. Jesus was constantly trying to make people believe in a God like that—a God Who wants His children to be strong and happy and do worthwhile work in the world—a Father Who is eager to put His love and wisdom at the call of any of His children at any minute."

We must begin by understanding our need to understand.

We think we know. The trail and the rocks and the ledges we think we know; it is an old story, centuries old; how can it hold any surprises now? It is old hat and full of fraud, some insist. A priest or parson or rabbi turns false to his vows and the cry goes up, forgetful of all the hundreds of thousands who remain true to those vows: "Look—that is what they are like. How could anyone believe what they preach when they act like that?"

Sometimes this certainty in our own infallibility has an almost amusing naïveté. The adolescent, the sophomore in college, debates with earnestness that excludes any possibility that he might be wrong. All is known, all is decided, all is written in the textbook. He knows, he has read it, he has heard it spoken by the great scholars.

Adolescent faith in the certainty of material

knowledge, of course, gets itself knocked about considerably in the university and the laboratory; we cannot go far on any road without being aware that much of what we *know* we only seem to know; much that we accept today we are compelled to denounce tomorrow.

Keats, full of sensate and spiritual reactions to the universe, wrote these lines:

Beauty is truth, truth beauty—that is all
Ye know on earth, and all ye need to know.

He was a very young man when he wrote those lines. Perhaps had Keats lived to be much older than he did—he was only twenty-five when he died—he might have given us in some later work, something even beyond these two magnificent lines of poetry. Could he have written, with equal sweep and certainty, the same words ten years later? Might not he have added that we need to know love, compassion, pity?

Keats himself put his confidence in emotions and experience. "Axioms in philosophy," he wrote in a letter to a friend, "are not axioms until they are proved upon our pulses. We read fine things but never feel them to the full until we have gone through the same steps as the Author—in fine, as Byron says, 'Knowledge is Sorrow,' and I go on to say that 'Sorrow is Wisdom'—and further for aught we can know for certainty 'Wisdom is Folly'! . . .

VISION

"I compare human life to a large Mansion of Many Apartments, two of which I can only describe, the doors of the rest being as yet shut upon me. The first we step into we call the infant or thoughtless Chamber, in which we remain as long as we do not think—We remain there a long while, and notwithstanding the doors of the second Chamber remain wide open, showing a bright appearance, we care not to hasten to it; but are at length imperceptibly impelled by the awakening of this thinking principle within us—we no sooner get into the second Chamber, which I shall call the Chamber of Maiden Thought, than we become intoxicated with the light and the atmosphere, we see nothing but pleasant wonders, and think of delaying there forever in delight: However among the effects this breathing is father of is that tremendous one of sharpening one's vision into the heart and nature of Man—of convincing one's nerves that the world is full of Misery and Heartbreak, Pain, Sickness and oppression—whereby this Chamber of Maiden Thought becomes gradually darkened and at the same time on all sides of it many doors are set open—but all dark—all leading to dark passages—We see not the balance of good and evil. We are in a Mist. We are now in that state—We feel the 'burden of the Mystery'. . . . Now if we live, and go on thinking, we shall explore them. . . ."

Whether we call them dark passageways in a Mansion of Many Chambers, or deep and hidden ravines of a mountain, it is an exploring of our own meanings and values and understandings, the sum total of our being, which is, in the final addition, the sum total of our faith.

On my desk is a golden watch, one of those large, old-fashioned hunting-case watches. It dates back to the last century and to an episode of faith—and of love.

My paternal grandmother was always a good Baptist. Her trust in God was very simple and basic and real. But the day came when even this trust was put to test.

My grandfather was manager of a streetcar line in Baltimore, Maryland, during the late years of the last century. A dispute had developed over some problem and the conductors announced they were not going to take out the cars. My father's father announced that he would take a car out himself because he did not believe that they had any just cause.

The men came to him and pleaded not to try. "We'll be there with bats and bricks and you'll be hurt or dead and the car smashed before you reach the corner," they warned.

He would not be intimidated. Nor would he listen to the pleading of my grandmother that she loved him more than she cared about his sense of duty and right and wrong.

All night she prayed that he would give up this

idea. Yet she was later to admit that in her heart she knew he would not; and she knew also, after hours in prayer, what she would do.

She prepared the breakfast and the warm bottle of milk for their infant son.

Alone, my grandfather went to the carbarn and pushed through the silent crowd of men that milled around the entrance. He got into a car and prepared to drive out. The doors were open and the men were waiting with their bricks and stones.

But before the car could start, its first passenger of that run climbed on board—a woman with a baby in her arms.

My grandfather looked in amazement at his wife and child. "Take the car out," she told him. "But we are going with you."

The bricks were ready as the car moved forward. But something stayed these men in their violence as they looked in bewilderment at the woman and infant. None dared to throw his stone.

The car went on its way, and made its appointed stops, and returned unhindered. By the time it returned the men were standing in small groups. Anger was gone from them. Perhaps each had seen in that woman and child, his own wife and child in the cab of the car.

Whatever the reason, they had managed to resolve their complaints in a discussion that was all but ended by the time the car returned. Instead of bricks, there were actually cheers as the car edged back into the barn.

And the men and management, glad that a possible prolonged dispute had been ironed out in less than two hours, presented my grandfather with a gold watch which I have now on my desk.

To my grandmother it was prayer that provided the answer. She asked His protection, she asked that things would work out all right. This was what she told me.

The individual petition of prayer is only one aspect of prayer's role in faith, and perhaps not the most essential. Again and again, the great religious leaders tell us in various ways that God already knows our needs; His goodness and kindness is already ours.

Then why do we pray? What do we pray for? What is prayer itself?

Prayer is a tuning in of our being with the Divine. It is a learning to listen, to understand, to merge with the Divine, to lose ourselves in the deep cooling waters of the universal soul. It is an articulation of gratitude for His strength and His blessing that is available to us. Prayer is not a particularizing or detailing of desires and hidden urges; it is an effort to effect the flow of power between the Self and the Divine.

It does not seek to utilize the Divine Will to its

specific purpose, but rather asks for the humility and understanding by which to adjust to that purpose, with perfect faith that the Infinite purpose is all-good, all-loving, all-forgiving, all-triumphant. Prayer is the affirmation of that triumph, it is gratitude for that purpose. It is adoration, in humblest and simplest terms, of the power and glory of the Creator.

Hallowed be Thy name.

It is as simple as this. We do not need high phrases, the great embroidery of praises, for all of this is known and what is in our heart can be said in only the basic words.

Prayer is no pounding on the gates of heaven with our puny fists; it seeks to change not the will of God, but ourselves, to make ourselves more fully the reflection of His perfection, to be more nearly the image and likeness of God.

We pray also to be the instrument of His will.

But we cannot always know in what way we may be taught to serve.

On a point of land where the Savannah River runs into the Atlantic, a woman lived alone in a small house. Years before, her sailor husband had gone to sea and failed to return. So certain was she that he was alive that she met every ship that came into the river, bound for Savannah docks. By day she waved a scarf, by night a lantern. Over the years she became a legend along the coast; cruise ships would awaken passengers to see the lantern of greeting through the dark.

Did she still believe her husband lived after all that time?

A captain of many years on merchant ships answered: "To every captain and crew coming into this river, it is a personal greeting. She is a symbol to each man—of love and faith waiting for them."

Every ship is her husband's ship and every sailor can share a portion of her faith.

Faith is not mere belief in supernaturalism; it is not mere trust in what Heaven or God can do for us. Faith requires more from us; it is also belief in truths on which all great religions have been built.

Above all, it is molded in love—love not of materiality but of God, love not in words and ritual but in fact, in using His gifts, in serving His world and His people.

14

PRECIPICE

The great corrosive factor is hate.

As we hate so we destroy—others, the world, ourselves.

As we hate our brother, so we hate ourselves, so we hate God.

For the God of vengeance died long since, but the God of love is eternal.

How can we hate and believe in Him?

A man clings to a girder, high above the river. A slip, a misstep, means certain death.

He has climbed out here to kill himself, and now police and clergymen and bystanders are trying to "talk him back from the brink of his self-decreed execution."

On this ledge between life and death, he discusses his problems with the clergymen. They do not seem to be very unusual or insolvable—except to him. One of these clergymen is a priest who brings out a

Bible and reads from the Book of St. Matthew, phrases about forgiveness:

"Then came Peter to him, and said, Lord, how oft shall my brother sin against me, and I forgive him? till seven times?

"Jesus saith unto him, I say not unto thee, Until seven times: but, Until seventy times seven. . . ."

The man on the ledge of eternity listens and sips coffee and talks. But as police and others creep close to him he angrily tells them to get back or he will jump.

The priest climbs out on the girder to talk with the man, who is still clinging to his precarious perch below the bridge railing. Police bring up emergency equipment.

It is Sunday afternoon. Thousands of cars are held up by this drama. A bridge official pushes through the crowd to see if the police won't get their equipment out of the way.

"You are holding up a million people," the bridge official states.

"I am trying to save a human being," the policeman answers.

The equipment remains, and the traffic jam grows worse.

Policemen hand the man on the girder more coffee and another cigarette, and the man and the priest talk on, about hate and love and forgiveness and guilt. This was no pulpit in some shadowed church, no book-lined quiet of the pastor's study, no psychiatric couch.

It was a human being brought to the point of self-destruction by self-hate, by his feeling that the world hated him and rejected him and wanted to destroy him, by his need to learn how to give—and receive—love.

We can call him and his action psychopathic, if we wish. We can say he was a show-off and a fraud who never intended to jump, but only wanted to call attention to himself and get publicity by stirring up trouble and interfering with the normal pursuits of Sunday afternooners.

We can say that we have no patience with him, or those like him; we can call them weaklings and misfits and tell them if they want to jump, go ahead. The world will be better off, we can insist.

But how wrong that will be! Of course, he was sick. He was sick with the virus revealed by such words as those above. The virus of rejection, of indifference, of dismissal—all varieties of the bleak emotion of hate. He was sick as a result of such viruses, sick to a point of death.

And a priest and a policeman and other strangers administered the first aid of caring for him; they applied a tourniquet of interest in him as a human being; as a creature who might even have a soul; they gave him resuscitation in terms of coffee and a cigarette against a backdrop of all the lifesaving equipment they brought up, police sirens and traffic stacked up for blocks.

It worked, finally, this therapy in limbo.

They talked him back to the world of life.

Did the others understand? His wife, his in-laws, his parents, his own physician? Particularly and above all his wife?

One cannot say. Perhaps what had happened would stand as an object lesson, and perhaps wise people would talk it over with her and the others around this man, and explain how hate manifests itself in a dozen different ways, often without the hater himself being aware, and how we have to fight against hate within ourselves, to aid other human beings, particularly those close to us, who need our love most.

To write of hate is to write of darkness. It is to turn, for a moment, into dark passageways, and chill, frightening shadows, and sharp-edged things we use, one against another.

But what has faith to do with hate? Why must we linger in this cold, bleak place to talk of these frightening shadows? Can we not turn to brighter things? This road to faith—is it not a highway full of flowers and gentle platitudes, as we were always led to think?

The subject of hate cannot be avoided, or by-passed; its presence in our lives is one of the virulent forces against which humans contend. In the measure that it is successful in permeating the walls of our being, in just so far, does it destroy and neutralize faith.

Let us look at this thing called hate, which is many things, actually, but let us stand our distance; keep clear of the showcases and do not touch the displays in this cavernous museum of the Fury; let us see what is here, but let us avoid being a part of it.

Here it is the child who hates her father; here is a mother who secretly and unknown, even to her innermost thoughts, hates her daughter, the child who took her beauty, the child who brought her pain, the child who stole the love of the father, the child who is the rival and competitor, the child who has youth and opportunity and future.

How many times, secret and unspoken and unrecognized, does it happen?

What life does not have a shadowed corner of hate that we could drag out and expose to public gaze? In one way or another it has affected us. And in one way or another we each try to escape or mitigate the results.

Here is a man who does not speak to a former friend. It is the man's judgment, his self-righteous condemnation of his former friend. The former friend does not return hate, does not desire to prolong resentment or anger. But efforts at a reconciliation through a go-between are summarily rebuffed.

This man who rebuffs any attempt at reconciliation with his friend considers himself a good Christian. On Sundays he goes to church. He works regularly with people in religious activities. He can recite the Nicene Creed with firm conviction.

It does not occur to him that this small action toward his friend has anything to do with religion or God or faith or the teachings of Christ.

"I have forgiven him, of course. Why shouldn't I forgive him? But why should I talk with him? I can forgive him, but I don't have to like him and I don't have to talk to him," he tells an acquaintance.

"In what way is your forgiveness shown?"

"Must I show it? Perhaps he is still committing the evil that made me break with him in the first place."

"Are you without evil yourself?" the acquaintance persists. "Have you the right to pass judgment on him, which could be mistaken? You could be wrong in your hate."

"Have I no right to my opinion?"

"Even a wrong opinion that hurts another?"

"I don't mean to hurt him. If my silence hurts him, it is his business, not mine."

His words scurry from corner to corner.

This is the great dilemma of the hypocrite. How do we reconcile our acceptance of the God of love—of forgiveness, of returning not only good for good but also good for evil—with hate, in whatever terms it is expressed?

PRECIPICE

Perhaps it is not a man we hate; perhaps it is a race, or a nation, a handful of people in another political party, people who believe differently than we do about the world or the universe, or people who have more money than we, or more power, and who use it ruthlessly for their own advantage? Unbidden and uncontrolled and self-righteous we cry out, "Isn't it right to hate such as these?"

The footless cliffs of hate, the overhanging resentment, the soaring peril of self-deceptions; these are the most dangerous and destructive areas to our lives —and our faith. Those who seek a road must climb above these escarpments or be thrown back and destroyed by them.

Hate, says the dictionary, is an emotion of intense aversion, usually springing from anger, fear or a sense of injury. Hatred, declares Professor Pitirim Sorokin of Harvard, is still "one of the most powerful emotions of man and one of the most efficient motors of human behavior."

Hateful behavior patterns may exist between individuals, or groups, or between an individual and the group. It may be open and recognized or disguised so that neither the hater or the hated is aware. It may be based on a known set of facts or conditions, on mere rumor or prejudice or merely on trying to stay in style.

Hate may be reasoned or unreasoned, deeply im-

§ 151 §

bedded or superficial, of long- or short-term duration; it may be the product of other deeply buried motives which must also be ferreted out; the mother-in-law who hates the girl who married her son, not for any of the open faults she finds with the young wife, but because this girl stole her son. Secret and deep runs this hate; and secret and deep run techniques often employed by the mother to injure without being openly discovered, even by herself. "I meant nothing by what I said, dear, really. You can't be so supersensitive all the time. . . ."

Should the wife learn to adjust to it, to accept and live with a constant stream of needle-jabs? The most probable answer is that the wife will seek to avoid the mother-in-law. So long as the mother hates, she stands to lose and to hurt even those she loves most. Conversely, as long as the daughter-in-law withholds forgiveness, she also loses.

The truth is that even in the act of leaving the object of our hate unnoticed, even in the process of "live and let live," we are nourishing the hate. The way to get rid of it is to love. And one way to love one's enemies is to forgive them. Fully and completely and unreservedly with no questions asked or stipulations made.

This was Jesus on the Cross, pleading the case of his executioners, asking the Father to forgive them, for they knew not what they did.

And if we have nothing to forgive, but if we

know after examination that it is our fault, at least in part, then it is we who must seek forgiveness and understanding, we must actively try to reconcile even the seemingly unreconcilable; there are actually no unreconcilable situations, even on the precipices of hate. There is a way through.

Love lies asleep sometimes in our hearts. Its force is unrecognized and unused because we use instead the clenched fist. All the way home from the office the husband recalls the bitterness of the morning quarrel with his wife, the selfishness of her attitude, the venom of her words; all the afternoon, while she shops and prepares dinner, the wife thinks of his ineptness, his lack of understanding, his concern only with his wants and desires; his rages and shouting at her, his coarseness. . . .

If thought has power at all, what are these two human beings doing by this mental cross fire? Can they go on living out their lives like this for the sake of propriety or religious scruples or whatever it may be that holds them together? Is the answer to be found in breaking up the home and the marriage or is it to be found in warring on hatred itself?

The conversion of hate into love is one of the great possibilities in the chemistry of the soul. This is a main reason for the almost universal appeal of Dickens's story, "A Christmas Carol." Scrooge is the symbol not of greed alone but essentially of hate; he hates Christmas because it symbolizes brotherhood, gift-giving and the joyous coming together of families in love—this is humbug, he insists. It is not the penny that he hordes but his carefully stacked up hate. And when his grueling experience reveals to him finally what he is doing to himself and what the end must be, hate is gone, replaced by self-realization translated into a belated love and he displays toward those around him, a love that wins him acceptance.

We think of Scrooge as the symbol of the miser. It was a miserliness not of money but of human affection. Scrooge is hate, bitterness, resentment perched on a barren stool. His escape comes by converting the paper-thin poverty of these emotions into the immeasurable wealth which is love.

Professor Sorokin insists that the only thing we can do with our hate is to convert its energy into new channels where it can do good: To drive it not at our fellow men, our relatives, or bride or betrothed, our brother or sister or ourselves, but at disease and evil and war and pain and ignorance and unhappiness. Channel it into the struggle against evil itself.

On a beach of northwest New Guinea a native woman lay wounded and bleeding. American corpsmen put her on a stretcher and carried her onto an LST where there was a doctor and an infirmary. She was seriously hurt. They did not know her name or whether she had been injured by our shells or by Japanese shells.

A medical officer on the ship toiled through the afternoon and the night to save her but it was of no use; in the dawn she was dead.

The LST was under way, plowing through the long swells of southern seas. On the deck of this LST a service was held. A young skipper—he was twenty-one or twenty-two—read from the Bible. Enlisted men and officers stood with heads uncovered in the bright equatorial sun. The body of the native woman lay on the deck, wrapped in white cloth.

It seemed so useless, her death. In its uselessness and its silent white-wrapped anonymity, it seemed to epitomize the meaning of war and hate, and their ultimate empty product.

"We don't know the woman's name," the captain said, "or what faith or religion she held.

"We do know that she was a casualty of war, an innocent bystander of battle.

"We do know that one of the main reasons we are fighting this war is to make it possible for innocent human beings anywhere in the world to live their lives out, peacefully and happily, without the fear of aggressors."

After a pause, "Heavenly Father, we commit this woman to Your care."

The sailors lifted the body and it slid from their grasp down into the sea. There was a splash and then silence.

This was the end product of aggression, violence,

war. This was the sum total of hate; the achievement of hate: To destroy guilty and innocent alike, friend and enemy alike.

How could one justify that dead woman whose body plunged down to that final splash in the sea?

We could not know. We could not answer. We could say this much: That we cared.

The men who carried her to the ship cared. The doctor who had fought with plasma and drugs to save her, the captain and officers and crew standing at this ceremony on the deck, cared.

To have faith we must love, and a part of love is to care and a part of caring is to take what action we can—for friend or foe or stranger who may cross our road.

Centuries ago, Jesus pointed out the road, mapped it precisely, so that any who wished to ascend these cliffs could follow His way.

"Ye have heard that it hath been said, An eye for an eye, and a tooth for a tooth:

"But I say unto you, That ye resist not evil: but whosoever shall smite thee on thy right cheek, turn to him the other also.

"And if any man will sue thee at the law, and take away thy coat, let him have thy cloak also.

"And whosoever shall compel thee to go a mile, go with him twain.

"Give to him that asketh thee, and from him that would borrow of thee turn not thou away.

"Ye have heard that it hath been said, Thou shalt love thy neighbor, and hate thine enemy.

"But I say unto you, Love your enemies, bless them that curse you, do good to them that hate you, and pray for them which despitefully use you, and persecute you;

"That ye may be the children of your Father which is in heaven: for he maketh his sun to rise on the evil and on the good, and sendeth rain on the just and the unjust.

"For if ye love them which love you, what reward have ye? do not even the publicans the same?

"And if ye salute your brethren only, what do ye more than others? Do not even the publicans so?"

We must love our enemy and salute him, we must do good to him and pray for him and bless him.

Out of doubting and questions and uncertainties, this road He points will take us up the sheer, sharp edge of the rocks.

We climb with the tools of forgiveness, pity, compassion, even sacrifice.

This is the route Christ charts for us across the face of hate.

15

PLATEAU

Sacrifice? To what and to whom? Do our modern gods, like their predecessors of another age, demand burnt offerings?

Sacrifice in modern faith is the outward sign of our inward caring. . . .

The dime in a beggar's cup, a moment of time for a caller in need, a letter to a friend or stranger, a word of kindliness to someone who does not matter to us.

It may be no more than this. Or it may be our life. . . .

Sacrifice is a symbol of acceptance of love of the Father and our brotherhood with all mankind.

We have scrambled and fought our way up precipices to the plateau above them; we make camp and light our fire and rest and prepare dinner in the dusk. The canvas lean-to gives us shelter against the wind, and through the narrow opening we can see the stars.

PLATEAU

We stare up at infinity and cannot understand it. Questions crowd in upon us. Astronomers are glib, with a hundred phrases—mass and gravitation and perimeters of the orbits, rotation velocities and density distributions. To the astronomer the universe is a familiar workshop, cluttered with specimens and samples and discards.

Yet the most powerful telescope reaches us only a little way, only to the edge of the back-yard fence, and what lies on the other side of the fence is speculation that only the most learned high priests of the sciences understand. It is a closed universe, they state. All space is curved, and parallel lines ultimately do meet. Our universe is really a vast amalgam of molecules, particles and masses of energy in a closed arena, something like the inside of a great cosmic globe.

What material binds this sphere? Of what is it composed? And what lies beyond? But scientists have postulated that there is nothing beyond and therefore, they answer, the question is impossible and cannot be asked.

But we have asked it and they do not answer.

We have asked these questions for thousands of years. The temple priests have given one reply and the priests of science another. Plato, in ancient Greece, speaks with the vast authority of the philosopher who knows all things:

"Time, then, and the heaven came into being at

§ 159 §

the same instant in order that, having been created together, if ever there was to be a dissolution of them, they might be dissolved together. It was framed after the pattern of the eternal nature . . . for the pattern exists from eternity, and the created heaven has been, and is, and will be, in all time. Such was the mind and thought of God in the creation of time. . . ."

Plato then briefly sketches how God created the planets and stars nearest the earth and assigned their proper orbits to earth. "To enumerate the places which he assigned to the other stars, and to give all the reasons why he assigned them, although a secondary matter, would give more trouble than the primary. These things at some future time, when we are at leisure, may have the consideration which they deserve, but not at present. . . .

"God lighted a fire, which we call the sun, in the second from the earth of these orbits, that it might give light to the whole of heaven. . . ."

We know how advanced was Plato's thinking in scientific terms for his era. Yet it is extraordinary that he was so sure of his answers; here and elsewhere he speaks with a certainty that allows no room for further discussion. The sun is there to light up the whole of the universe; he has spoken and this is the answer. From where does he derive this indisputable information? How can Plato be certain that the sun *is* the center of the universe?

There is a tragic factor in the realization that

Plato, who gave the world so much, was also mistaken in so much of what he presented as indisputable fact, particularly in regard to the creation of the earth and the stars and human beings. For if this tremendous mind could not perceive the possibility of error in his findings, what of our modern scientists and thinkers, our physicists and chemists and astronomers and nuclear scientists? Is it not possible that they, too, along with vast discoveries that are entirely correct and workable, also have put forth theories which will be found as profoundly incorrect, from a factual point of view, as those of Plato?

Science and materialism in general have indeed reached their own plateau, a platform in space itself, and our question comes: Have they found all answers —or any—this way? Will we be led ultimately to discard the spiritual universe when we discover that we are living in a vast goldfish bowl beyond which lies a perfected nothingness of which we cannot even conceive at present?

Is this to be the final achievement of man—the cosmic discovery of his own lack of purpose?

Or is there the possibility of other meanings and other interpretations about which, in many cases, some of our newer scientists appear almost totally unconcerned?

There are many plateaus. One may be a level achieved in a business or profession. It may be a financial or personal level of achievement—owning a certain dress or coat or car, living in a certain home or apartment house or down a certain street.

Each achieves his plateaus in a different way—personally, philosophically, spiritually. To one man it is belonging to the country club; to the next it may be meeting and talking with some celebrity, or being asked to make a speech, or to take over a committee chairmanship.

To others the plateau is security; the job that cannot be lost, the unassailable protection no matter what, the pension, the political appointment, the made-work job offered by a relative who happens to own the factory.

To some it is simply money. For others, all that counts is what is achieved by attention-getting devices. Stand on the plateau and beat the drums and strut the stage in a new mink coat.

In both the materialistic and spiritual senses, there are those who accept the plateau as the full realization beyond which they neither desire nor attempt to progress, and there are those to whom the plateau is only a way station.

The greatest of our scientists and thinkers did not stop, but plunged on. Plato, dogmatic or not, was such. And St. Augustine. And Thomas Aquinas. And Edison who might have stopped when he gave electric light to the world, but who kept on with his experiments and discoveries all his life, and in his last years was engaged in some extraordinary experiments on the nature of the soul in its relationship to the physical being.

We reach the plateau, whatever it may be in our lives, largely, we believe, because of our own merits, or our good fortune which we probably deserved. We have done it, we are here. We are proud—rightly proud, we say—of our achievement.

Ours?

We want the glory and we forget our own impermanence as physical beings; the self struggles for its glory too often without thought of God or His strength or the possibility of its own nothingness without Him.

Here is a woman who plays the piano as few on earth; her gift is deep and real; millions are stirred and transported by her music.

But she lives for herself, she lives for the money she earns, she lives for her own glory as expressed in this talent.

It is not enough. Talent remains, but her personal life withers, the parasite of self twines around her gift and crushes her strength.

She plays on. Her concerts continue to be heard, but gradually she begins to fade; nothing is wrong with her ability, she plays with the same fingers and skill, but not with the same soul, one guesses.

She is breaking up with her husband, we hear;

she has another man, a string of men; she is living in Paris; or is it Cannes? She is back in America; now she is fat, she is drinking; she is still a great artiste; she will tell you that herself. But it is not so. . . . Self has won and stands strident on its own barren, crumbling plateau.

If we would gain ourselves, we must first lose ourselves.

We meet a minister of God who has done well. He knows his theology and his congregation; their weaknesses and strengths, richness and poverty. He is a good pastor and his voice booms out the sermon and the prayers.

Yet there are a dozen places in his parish where he could, if he wished, take action. And where he withholds his courage and his gifts of persuasion because he sees no reason to move into the situation.

Let well enough alone, he decides. This is a good church, and the problem of whether we let in Puerto Ricans or Negroes or Chinese is not one in which we have to become involved.

"Let the vestry worry about it," he tells his wife.

And she nods, because here on this high plateau, with its stained-glass windows and its high steeple, the universe is sweet, she thinks, and safe.

The strength of the universe is around us; we must reach out to it and in reaching we must learn to forget ourselves. We plunge ahead, heedless of self. There is a recklessness in divinity that calls to us, a fantastic impracticability. It is this message that we see scrawled in the stars, splashed across the heavens.

Even in the midst of the evil of war, this spirit is found.

It may be in the deed of some general that is widely publicized, or in the acts of some individual whose name you rarely hear.

"Wilkie" was one of the latter type. His real name was Wilkins. Long before the Second World War Wilkie wanted to be in the Army. He applied for an appointment to West Point and would have made it except for two crooked front teeth.

What kind of general would he ever make, with two crooked front teeth?

But when the war broke out, Wilkie went into the Army Air Force as a pilot on a medium bomber. The "Grim Reapers" lived up to their name, for themselves and the enemy. They sank more tonnage than a dozen other squadrons—and their casualties were 3,000 per cent. Wilkie was with them all the way, up from Australia and across the New Guinea jungles.

He was still in his early twenties when they made him squadron commander. As the "old man," he called the flyers together and told them he would lead every mission personally. It was said that Wilkie lived for his men and fought for them and seemed to die when one of them died.

It was too much for any youngster. Commanding

officers finally told him: "You've had it, Wilkie. We know about the girl in Australia you're planning to marry. Go on down and take yourself a honeymoon."

There was one more mission, over a half-forgotten piece of South Pacific jungle island called Rabaul, an enemy base at that time.

They had expected no real trouble. But the enemy had changed his defenses and brought in new guns and the sky suddenly was full of exploding death. There was no time to halt the raid, to go higher, to pull the flyers out in time.

Wilkie had made his own bomb run; he could have gotten away. But the others were behind him— they also had families and sweethearts.

Two cruisers at the mouth of the harbor were sending up a barrage. None of the planes would get through that wall of death. Wilkie turned. He headed his own planes back and he dove directly at the cruisers, drawing their concentrated fire.

He could not hurt the enemy. His own bombs had already been dropped. But his action enabled the others in his squadron to run the gantlet to safety, out to the open sea.

Wilkie's death in that hell raining up from Japanese cruisers was no empty defeat, no cringing on some plateau of security, waiting for nothingness.

It was the willingness to move on, to risk, even to sacrifice, for an unspoken faith that reached beyond the terror of the moment.

He gave his life, in that split second of decision, not to die, but to live.

> *Greater love hath no man, Jesus said, than that he lay down his life for his friend.*
>
> *Rarely, indeed, is the sacrifice demanded by love so great as this.*
>
> *But demand there is, surrender there is, self-denial there is, sacrifice there is.*
>
> *However great or small, planned or un-planned, the sacrifice we make for our brother is the outward symbol of inner certainty.*
>
> *We ask no return and seek none.*
>
> *For whatever is our need, we know, will be fulfilled.*

16

BREAD OF LIFE

*However high we may reach in our journey,
our findings are empty if they are without application in our lives.*

*This does not mean to parade our faith before
others, like a new suit of clothes.*

It is not to seek to force others to our way.

*It is rather, to live what we have learned, to
make it truly ours.*

An Australian youth went to England with his
regiment in the First World War. Thousands of miles
from his homeland, he found the English people
warm and hospitable; they took him into their homes.

When, during the Second World War American
troops began landing on Australian soil, under the
command of General MacArthur, this man and his
wife found a chance to pay back his debt. They decided to open their home, on the outskirts of Brisbane, to any American GI looking for a meal, a bath,
a night's lodging, or a week's rest or two.

They asked no money for this. They and their

daughters, one seventeen and the other much younger
—their son was away in the Australian Air Force—
wanted only to return the kindness the father himself
had received, years before, in another war, thousands
of miles from his home.

In the course of the war in the Pacific, nearly
a hundred American boys, from almost every state,
stayed in this home. Many would come back on leave
or furlough, for a few days or a week or two, from
New Guinea or Biak or some other point "up north."
The mother was "Mom" and the girls were "Sis" and
the father "Dad."

For many of these boys this became a second
home. They could lounge in the living room, or forage
in the icebox, or sit and talk, or sleep, or read a book in
the night. They could talk about home and family or
war experiences or girl friends.

Home, someone once wrote, is a place that when
you get there, they can't send you away.

This Australian family made theirs that kind of
home.

It would have been so easy to be frightened. How
could they know, or the Australian Red Cross volun-
teers who often sent the GI's along know, who these
boys were? How could anyone be sure they were not
thieves or potential murderers or rapists?

In a war, all kinds of men are drawn into an
army, and war brings out the good—and sometimes
the worst—in man.

Much of the time, the mother and the two girls were alone in the house with their assortment of "guests."

But nothing happened in all that time, with any of those boys who came into their home, often just back from the front, unshaven and without fresh clothes; sometimes sick with malaria or dysentery, sometimes grown so thin he could hardly be recognized as the boy who had left for the jungles up north, a year or so before.

Once Noel, the oldest girl, was coming home on the local train when she saw three American Marines. They apparently were just coming back from the jungles. Noel, with almost alarming directness, asked them, "How would you Yanks like to have a bath?"

They looked at her in sober silence for an instant. Finally, one of them countered tentatively, "A real bath? With *real* hot water?"

Noel nodded.

They looked at each other again. The spokesman said, "We've got an overnight pass, that's all. We've got to be on our way back tomorrow. If we could get a good hot bath with hot water for a start—boy, that would be living."

One of the others said, "Well, what do we do now?"

Noel said, "Just follow me. We get off the next station."

§ 170 §

Wordlessly, the three Marines followed the girl off the train and up the few blocks to her home. The parents and several of their GI "family" were at dinner. Noel called out, "Hi, folks. I've brought home three Yanks. They want a bath."

The mother called out, "Fine. Be sure they have soap and towels."

The flabbergasted Marines went upstairs to bathe. They came downstairs a half hour later, washed and shining. By that time cake and coffee were ready for them—American-style coffee, made in a Silex that one of the boys had had his mother ship from the States.

Afterward, as they left, one of the Marines was heard to comment, "That's the dog-gondest pickup I ever had or hope to have as long as I live."

After the war, the parents made a trip to America and visited every city where their boys lived, stopping to call and say hello, and meet the wives and children and the mothers and fathers of their small army of foster sons, and reminisce about their Brisbane "home away from home."

They did not think of what they had done as any great act. They simply did it out of their desire to help repay a debt.

Faith is not faith unless we give it a definition in action, unless and until we translate abstract religious formalism into concrete meaning, and recognized debt into our conscious deed.

There is sincerity that goes beyond words. It does not ask praise, it does not demand recompense; it returns good for good as well as good for evil, without expectation.

What is our real purpose deep within ourselves? The good opinion of our fellow men? Or the integrity of our relationship to the Almighty, in the secret pact between Him and us?

That was the key to the lives of that man and woman, reaching out with warmth as stand-ins for mothers and fathers far away.

It was only a handful of boys who came to their home and lolled in their living room and their kitchen, in a place called Brisbane, Australia, and laughed and joked and for a moment forgot the war.

But in its way it was the whole issue of that terrible struggle, the whole underlying conflict— whether a handful of human beings, or even one, was important, not for rank or wealth or name, but only and entirely because he was the child of the universe.

Only we—and God—can gauge the depth of our sincerity.

For faith to be effective in us, we must seek to believe with our whole being—mind, heart, body, spirit, the totality of Self.

To translate this seeking into action, we must reach out to God's universe, we must give as He gives to us, as He wants to give to us if we will but open the channels of faith.

Demand no payment in kind.

Do not expect rewards.

Give freely of your bread, rejoicing only in the awareness of God's love, in the doing of His work.

This is the spiritual nucleus from which all else flows.

17

FOREST

The high hazard of hypocrisy looms for the insincere, for all who falsely pretend holiness.

The road is steep, the turning sharp, the edges sheer, the encircling woods dense and full of deceptive shadows.

The forest of the hypocrite is a place of snares and traps and shivering naked things that too often are semblances and echoes of ourselves and our deeds and words.

It is an unexpected place, the forest of ice. It is the product of avalanche and wind and storm, the spilling down of glacier masses and rocks, rumbling and roaring and piling up here at the foot of the northern face of the mountain, a grotesque unearthly forest of weird contorted forms, a waxworks of nature's humor and horror.

It is a world of pretense. In each of these forms we seem to see representatives of our world, our lives and ourselves. They seem almost real, but they are not—they are only shapes in snow and ice, lifeless things that lean with the winds of the mountain or crackle at night like moonlit spectres.

The ice forest of sham and hypocrisy is a place of special attractions. A beguiling place that lures one on, from one shape to the next, one grotesque to another, one sham further until we are lost and run from this one to that, seeking our road.

We can have no faith if we are trapped in such a place, or by such ideas. Hypocrisy itself is a corroding force that withers whatever it touches, wherever it takes hold, no matter how good or valuable. The hypocrite digs his own grave.

Here is a twisted thing of ice, melted and frozen, remelted and reshaped a thousand times by nature, by below-zero nights and blazing days.

This one is like a man; big, blustery, with rumpled hair, an orator on a stump, a politician pleading for a vote. Honesty, integrity, liberalism, conservatism and middle-of-the-roadism, all at once. He is for all that is good and against all that is bad.

There are those who say he does not tell the truth. There are stories of fifty-thousand-dollar pay-offs and payments taken for appointments after his election. There are those who say that behind the high-sounding words of the politician is a mass of lies. We glance up, but the silent form gives no response.

Here is the ice figure of a woman, head high,

chest flung out. There are ladies on church committees who look like her. Her work and her contributions are needed. She has given much of her time and effort, enjoying it because this committee work makes her a part of the swim of things. She has power in her little world and wields it with a master's touch. She knows all her fellow workers and her memory has ticketed all their weaknesses; and sometimes she rides roughly over the prostrate forms of other ladies of the committee.

Deep down she wants to believe in a conventional God. She wants to be sincere. But behind the ice-blue exterior, she is forever at war with other demanding forces, pride and envy and malice, scandalmongering and character assassination on a ladylike basis.

The ice-blue figure seems to billow and bustle in the mountain winds. . . .

Here is another—the form of a man whose head is bowed. A long lean bean pole of a man. An intellectual giant, looming above us, looking down upon us. "God?" he seems to cry. "Why tell me of God? I am interested in men, in people, in the sinews and sufferings and significance of man. I'm too busy to waste time."

"You don't believe in Him?"

"It would be sophomoric to say we do not believe. It is sophomoric to give Him attributes. We serve Him by serving man, by serving ourselves."

High above us his lanky figure towers, long arms seeming to dangle at his icy sides. How many are there who beg the metaphysical question with a humanist plea?

A man lectures on life's underdogs and finds fortune and fame as their spokesman. But when he is asked to work with a group of these same men, he is too busy. He has not time for them personally, he explains.

His time and effort lecturing at a top-drawer price constitute his gift to them.

And he lives off the fat of their hunger.

He is not real, of course. He is only a looming, symbolic thing in ice. . . .

The forest is a place of twisted shapes, of figures bowing and cringing, of contorted ideas and ritualistic poses:

A woman with a child. She goes to church regularly, but her child will not play with Catholics or Jews. Christianity is all right, but there are other factors, are there not?

Or a man of the church. He cares more for the money a widow will give than for her grief.

Or a woman who pretends almost to saintliness. But in her heart she hates her husband and with her soft words she seeks to destroy him.

Or this contorted man who pretends to love, but whose life is one long chain of lies and adulteries.

The road winds on through this museum and we

find suddenly that we are looking not at strangers or twisted shapes, but in some measure at ourselves.

Are we then hypocrites?

The possibility seeps into our awareness.

How much do we contribute to hypocrisy? we wonder. How many times have we bowed in prayer but have not prayed? How many times have we hated deep inside when we said we loved? How many times do we go through the rituals of kindness and mean it not at all? How many times have we had a friend who trusts us, but we ourselves know that we are not his friend, that we do not like him or trust him or believe him? How many times have we talked one way and meant another, because it was expedient to do so; talked one way and voted another, because it was diplomatic to do so; talked one way and wished another, because we thought it was wise; prayed one way and talked another, because it seemed practical?

How many times have we judged without mercy while preening ourselves upon our merciful nature; how many times have we washed and cleaned and polished the outside of the cup and the platter and allowed the corroding filth of extortion and excess and greed to remain and spread on the inside; how many times do we make ourselves like the whited sepulchres of which Jesus speaks?

This is the forest of strange shapes, a forest that gleams and softens and melts away in the sun because it cannot abide the light or warmth. But in darkness and shadows it takes a deceptive and misleading form.

It is the forest peopled too often by ourselves.

And in whatever measure we contribute to its sham—we have abandoned faith. God is not deceived, and faith in Him which does not accept also the proper laws of His universe is meaningless.

The forest is a scrub growth of human weakness, the product of rebellion and betrayal of the love of God.

There is no map through this world of misshapen things. The route exists in our own minds and hearts or not at all. The challenge is within us, whether we can go ahead or not, whether we climb or not.

The answer is not in the road or in this forest, in books or rituals or sermons; it can be found only within ourselves, and what we really mean about life and about God, and how deeply we strive to mean these things.

Our belief calls for the honesty to face weaknesses where they exist, to admit them and to seek to grow from that point. Faith that puts on fancy words to cover empty meaning is not faith at all but mockery.

The forest is chill and lonely and whimpering in the night.

Hurt and love. Guilt and innocence. Your father

and his faith. His was different from yours, but now you know it does not matter that it was different because all faith is the same, the great pool of faith from which we draw our strength is the same; only our understanding is different.

The law changes not, the meaning changes not, only we change, only we learn, only we grow. For there is no difference that matters if we have found our faith; we are all subject to the same God and the same law; ritual and formalism are only that, but the truth is truth.

And we must know ourselves—our weaknesses and our failings and our shortcomings. We must know that we at times have sinned mightily against God and man and ourselves, against every living being; there can be no help for this except in God and in His forgiveness.

For the restoring of the soul comes only with the cleansing of the spirit.

"Thou hypocrite," the mind cries out.

And alone in the church a man kneels and bows his head and weeps. And prays.

18

LEDGE

The ego is but a fragment of infinity.

If we think we have reached our goal, we almost surely have not.

If we imagine we have found the sole route to God, we almost certainly have found no route.

If we imagine ourselves above all others, we are certainly below them all.

For vanity is wine and pride is blazing sun, but humility is the cooling wind and rain of the soul.

Above the forest, along the steep trail, we reach the ledge, and pitch our tent in the face of gale winds against the rocks. We rest and sleep, in this precarious perch, only a few feet from where the sheer mountain face plunges down hundreds of feet.

Tonight there are no stars and outside there is only the incessant haranguing of the wind against the canvas. We cling to our perch and snatch moments of sleep.

THE ROAD TO FAITH

The skies lighten. Below us the daybreak mist lies like a blanket over the earth, rumpled and worn. Above the mist, sky colors change in a symphony of golds and violets and grays.

This is a moment of truth before us in the elements of the out-flung pattern.

We have reached a level of spectacular views and spectacular possibilities. We have attained a point higher than we had imagined we could.

What are the implications of this moment and of this height—and of the route beyond?

It is clear to us now that faith is not one thing but many things, not a monolithic fact but a multitude of ingredients, not a homogenous quality apart from other qualities, but a sum total of all our qualities, all our notions, all our being.

It is certainty of the love and benevolence of the Creator, of our ability to reach out to that benevolence and to make ourselves a part of its strength if we truly and firmly seek. It is certainty that we can find the way. Faith is the achievement of inner glory as dizzy and overpowering as this gold-spun vista of mountain dawn.

We have reached a point where some if not all of the meaning clarifies. We begin to realize that we are reaching toward a concept of the wholeness of things, to a groping and as yet incomplete comprehension of the Absolute.

§ 182 §

The mists fluff across the earth below us in their patterns, and patches of green fields merge with the pale blues and whites of the mists themselves.

Have we understood then that faith is not a thing only of the mind but of the soul, not a skill to be learned in a laboratory, but also at an easel or before a grand piano or in front of a blank piece of paper on which we scrawl words? In his book, *Let Go and Let God,* Dr. Albert E. Cliffe tells his readers:

"For ages religion has been looked upon as a science rather than an art. We have taught it in precepts, in dogmas, and in creeds, not in realities, not in absolute faith. Since the second century man has, through the church, formed varying dogmas differing from century to century. . . . Let us all try to find this Christ within so that we may all worship Him in spirit and in truth and that He may so fill our hearts that we all worship together in spite of our so-called differences."

To achieve faith is not to acquire a set of rules that we memorize, but a full heart which we accept with joy. It is to open our beings to the flooding power of the Infinite. It is to know the fullness of holy spirit that pervades and affects every action of our lives.

It is love for others, for strangers we do not know; it is caring about those strangers and being willing to go to their aid, even to the extent of making them our personal responsibility.

It is willingness to act not only for self but also

for the unself, for the good of an infinitude of other souls, throughout the world and worlds undiscovered throughout creation.

It is willingness to love and a recognition of our own need and our own limitations; we are mortal, we are not God, and we cannot know or guess all of His purposes, and we have no road maps of heaven. In all humility we must admit that we do not know these things; the secrets of the universe are God's and not ours.

We can recognize our limitations and strive within them to fulfill the will of God as He gives it to us to understand.

We can recognize that each of us must find his way by his own lights, and that what is truth for one man may not be truth for someone else; as the colors on the mist may seem different from one individual to the next, and who is there to say that each is not correct, by his own sights?

There is a sense of peace in this beginning of understanding. It permeates our being in the midst of hectic hours, of turmoil and strife and need; in the midst of the battle for existence, for a dollar, for position, power, prestige, there is a surging of peace.

It may come—at this level of faith—in many ways, suddenly, swiftly, or in a measured pace that does not reach our conscious awareness until moments or hours later.

This sense of peace emerges not as escape from reality, but as reality itself. The clamor of the world, the shouting of the competition, the blare of the advertisers, the complaints of the boss and the nagging of a hundred petty harassments appear in their true unreality.

There is something more, we are aware—a reality beyond the immediacy of these things close at hand; a reality—a dimension—of a wholly different kind.

The drive of men to reach a purity of faith, stripped of the violence and insensibility and paradoxical contradictions one finds in so many orthodoxies, has groped its way across history.

Now defeated, now turned down false roads and misused, now thrown to earth in the midst of riot and war and bath of blood, it rises and keeps on. The urge, the intuition, the need, is too strong for mankind itself to defeat.

In ancient Greece there was a multiplication of pagan deities, whose mythical abode was on Mt. Olympus, and whose actions, both moral and immoral, mirrored realistically the actions and weakness, good and evil, foibles and cruelties, kindness and rugged individualism of the Greeks themselves. It is a trait of man in early spiritual development to endow his God with those traits he himself possesses—thereby hoping to excuse his own failings and glorify his own virtues.

Yet even at the height of Greek paganism, we find glintings of another approach entirely, a prompting in a totally different direction. For example, Xenophanes, writing in the sixth century before Christ:

"Homer and Hesiod have ascribed to the gods all things that are a shame and a disgrace among mortals, stealings and adulteries and deceivings of one another. . . .

"But mortals deem that the gods are begotten as they are, and have clothes like theirs, and voice and form.

"Yes, and if oxen and horses or lions had hands, and could paint with their hands, and produce works of art as men do, horses would paint the forms of the gods like horses, and oxen like oxen, and make their bodies in the image of their several kinds.

"The Ethiopians make their gods black and snub-nosed; the Thracians say theirs have blue eyes and red hair.

"The gods have not revealed all things to men from the beginning, but by seeking they find in time what is better.

"One god, the greatest among gods and men, neither in form like unto mortals nor in thought. . . .

"He sees all over, thinks all over, and hears all over.

"But without toil he swayeth all things by the thought of his mind.

"And he abideth ever in the selfsame place, moving not at all, nor does it befit him to go about now hither now thither. . . ."

Throughout Greece, during the age of its greatest achievement, and later in Rome as well, wise men and leaders and poets like Xenophanes sought through various groups and religious-philosophical approaches to reinterpret the myths of the gods in terms of the spirit and its role in the individual life.

The opposition came, as it so often does, from orthodoxy, entrenched behind both religious and political fortifications and determined, if possible, to destroy any threat to the old ideals. Many of the leaders of ancient Greek thought were urging a return to the ancient gods of Olympus who were worshiped more and more in form only but not in spirit.

At the same time, when schools such as Eleatic and the Ionic sought to bring to the fore the new idea of the One Supreme Being, and when the "rational mythologists" tried to reinterpret the myths in terms of morality and spiritual symbolism—they brought upon themselves attacks, denouncements and even death.

They were striving, these few, to bring faith into reality in their own time and land. It was a true faith, as they understood it. Faith in a Supreme Being, a God of truth, of love, of morality. They had found a road for themselves even in that day.

Men have always sought the road according to their own lights. The early church sought it in the catacombs and secret congregations, keeping alive the story of Jesus and the Resurrection and the miracles of Christ.

New England Pilgrims sought it on a small vessel crossing to an unknown land. The Quakers sought it even amid persecution. The Mormons sought it by trekking across the wilderness of America.

The Navaho Indians of New Mexico and Arizona were called primitive, and our anthropologists studied them and their tribal rites as specimens of a well-developed but still primitive culture. Yet read, from one of their prayers:

Oh, male-divinity!
With your moccasins of dark cloud, come to
us. . . .
In beauty I walk.
With beauty before me, I walk.
With beauty behind me, I walk.
With beauty below me, I walk.
With beauty above me, I walk.
With beauty all around me, I walk. . . .
It is finished in beauty.

But there are other aspects of the Navaho and his culture. Sculptress Malvina Hoffman, in her book, *Heads and Tails*, describes a Navaho Indian ritual:

"In San Felipe we witnessed the corn and rain dance. . . . The grouping of the Indians in costume, chanting and dancing to the rhythmic pounding of the tom-tom, was a most brilliant affair. The blazing sun added a certain splendor to the swaying lines of glistening, brown bodies and waving pine boughs, and the breeze blew their long, black hair around their shoulders. Two groups . . . kept up a continual rhythmic intonation and invocation for rain, hour after hour, until sunset. A leader carried a long pole, ending in a bunch of corn leaves. This he waved over the heads of the dancers, shaking out the sacred pollen and calling the rain to shed its benediction on the seeded earth. On our way home the heavens darkened and a thunderstorm came. . . ."

An answer from Heaven in response to a savage dance—or a coincidence?

We cannot know or guess. Yet we may assume that purity of spirit, on a level high above mere primitive superstition in ritual only, was in their prayer.

The mists below us roll on.

The world lies naked now, it seems, sprawled at the foot of our mountain, across space and across time.

And here is an army of mankind, reaching back to Eden, reaching back to the caves and jungles.

Mistaken and misguided and misdirected, greedy for plunder and power, for self-glorification, marching to kill and to maim, judging in rashness and punishing in vengeance, burning at the stake, forcing con-

fessions from the innocent, torturing and murdering
and burning human beings to death in the name of
God.

This also we have achieved—this badge of violence. For we are part of the calvalcade, we are a part
of this species.

That is why we may say, here upon our mountain, that it was for us that He died upon His cross,
and it was for us that He pleaded the forgiveness of
the Father.

Beyond us and around us this army of humanity
surges forward toward its goal. We stumble and falter
and fall back and push on.

But in this struggle we have not given up our
quest for the good and we have not surrendered to
our weakness and evil and betrayal of our own cause.

We have not surrendered and we have pleaded
again and again on our knees for forgiveness and we
have risen to our feet and started once again along
this road.

We and those around us, this long, searching
army of humanity that seems to reach back to the rim
of time.

*We must accept ourselves with all our weak-
nesses and strengths.*

*We must accept others equally, with their
weaknesses and strengths.*

All others. All the created beings of God, it

matters not what race, what color, what creed, we must accept as we accept ourselves.

In acceptance, in humility, we learn to let our love reach out to all things, all beings of every nation, of every world, to all the divine flowing stream of eternal life.

been driven is loosened; the climber finds himself dangling above nothingness, hands clawing the air.

But he does not fall. The man above holds firm, holds with courage and incredible strength and calls down reassuring words. The dangling man is swung back to a secure grip on the rock face.

The moment is past and the seemingly endless seconds in which he dangled above eternity are over. The man above grins and the group moves on.

Part of faith in God resides in our faith in other human beings, in the children of His creation. Part of our faith must rest upon our brotherhood with all men, and the interdependence of all mankind. Part of our faith is our awareness that what happens to other human beings anywhere on earth is in a measure happening to us; that when they triumph over evil, we share in that triumph; when they lie crushed and broken, we also share in their pain.

Without this sense of oneness and attunement with our fellow man, oneness and attunement with God is difficult and perhaps impossible. There are those who may go alone long distances and to great heights; ultimately they find themselves in high and bleak emptiness, peopled with pallid echoes. Often in such moments they reach out for help, for neighbors and friends, for relatives, for love.

And suddenly they become aware that their interdependence is a pleasurable and exciting aspect of their faith; they do not need to lock and bolt all the doors of their lives to keep out invaders; they do not need to set up walls between themselves and others; they do not need to be afraid to chat with strangers; the world is their brother and sister—the weak and strong, the Negro, the Chinese, the white man, the hoodlum, the thief.

Not only are they brothers, but they discover that they are dependent on each other, and failure to recognize this interdependence would be an omission of profound importance.

This is particularly true when we have reached a level well above our starting point, when we have attained understanding in spiritual terms regarding the ways by which faith is won. At this level, errors become costly; the achievement of this height brings with it responsibility. What might have been brushed aside as trivial at a lower stage assumes greater significance here; a stumble below could have brought scratches and bruises, at a higher point it could bring almost irretrievable disaster.

We are brothers, children of the great Cosmic Being. We share this dependence and love; it is in this context that our lives merge.

The man below on the line gives a cry of pain. He has twisted his foot in the crack of rock to which he clings. While he tries to free the foot, the others in the group wait, poised in their perilous positions against the sheer rock.

He calls up that he will cut the rope and go on down. But his foot is caught and we tell him to wait. We are frightened, terrified, and yet not surrendering to fear; we are recalling one man who was not afraid and whose lack of fear saved us only moments before.

This is the example: Every single man on that rope is together. And so we lower and bend down and we reach out and free his foot.

It is a minor incident, but it is important to us because it makes us feel that brotherhood as an integral part of faith is no longer merely a word but a reality.

And so a band of strangers—and brothers—moves on. It works its way upward along the high face of the mountain, above the sea of clouds, above the world, torn between doubt of ever achieving the goal and certainty of achieving it.

The winds of many doubts blow against our faces, with chilling currents that sweep down upon us, swirling and plunging and challenging; there are mighty gusts filled with a thousand reasons why we have no right to our peak of faith, why we must be turned back from our objective, whipped back to earth.

Our ministers and priests and rabbis know how difficult is this way of the average man or woman to faith, how often the layman is flung back, how often the world intrudes its jutting edges of so-called "realities" that spin us downward.

It is a pastor's daily round to see these things, to provide comfort and strength and help where he can, particularly to those of the great army of seekers with all their questions and doubts.

One such pastor and priest, the Reverend John Ellis Large of New York's Church of the Heavenly Rest, in a book entitled *Think on These Things,* wrote these words:

"It's this steady taking of one step at a time—in worshipful acts of faith unproved as yet, and with no discernible end ever in sight—which ultimately leads to that perfect trust which wipes out all fear from even the deepest recesses of life. And though every man must, in the last analysis, face his own crises alone, the inner struggle for the facing of them comes most adequately from within the fellowship of the faithful. . . ."

Do not be afraid to talk with God, and to let Him talk to you.

For you will know then the experience of God in your life, and your faith will begin to shape itself in His reality.

You will know His voice in the quiet.

And your answer will come, perhaps then, or in some way you cannot know, but it will come, like the unfolding of the flower.

"But the answer may be only in my mind, and it is only coincidence, is that not so?" you ask.

Wait.

THE ROAD TO FAITH

Wait even in the darkest forest.
And listen in the silence that is also a part of
the vastness of His creation.
And you will know.

20

VOICES

Listen: The voices of disbelief are taunting, deriding, making mockery.

Do we stop up our ears? Shout back in fury? Lash at them with whips? Order their arrest as heretics?

We cannot be the judge of anyone, we in our cloak of faith, old or new.

For we are not God, but His children, and these are our brethren, even these who cry out to us and seek to tear Him from our lives.

Their cries, their denunciations, their misunderstandings and misinterpretations call for answers.

But we answer only in compassion, in the terms of the temperate, the controlled, the godly.

Out of wind-swollen clouds, out of jagged wisps of fog that run like ghosts across the sky, out of howling storm and pelting ice come strident voices, challenging, demanding, taunting.

We have reached thus far, but our hold is tenuous and around us storm strikes; and the crawling things, and carping things, the snide voices of doubt, pursue and nag and lunge.

Some of these voices seem near, some far off; the cries of some who fell or surrendered or never dared, of some who turned away in hatred and momentary defeat and rage—and of those who for a handful of silver would seek to sell out God Himself.

A thousand ideas, a thousand challenges, cry out of the storm and the winds.

On the edges we hear the chatter of disbelief, a litany of the doubters, an endless jabber that offers little or nothing but seeks to destroy whatever we have:

"Faith ought to be against the law."

"Do you swallow that pap about loving your enemies and turning the other cheek?"

"It's in our minds. We create God in the image and likeness of our father and mother. That's what. . . ."

"And how do you know there is anything beyond? You don't know. I say when you're dead, you're dead. We're a chemical accident."

"The mind? What is it? Stick a pin in the human brain and what happens? You may radically alter the mind and the soul, whatever that is."

"There is so much we can't find out. . . ."

"Don't give me any of that religious stuff, for God's sake. . . ."

The voices emerge and grow loud and die away; they are on every side of us, a cosmic cocktail hour of disillusioned chatter.

The voices and their derisions and impieties claw at us. The voices are many. Their variety is diverse; each is sure of itself and each must destroy us because a true disbeliever is a lonely man and needs to share his disbelief.

"And is your God always there? Does He take occasional vacations?"

"Stop that——"

"Listen," the voice persists. "A man is sick, and the doctor says he will die. Nothing can save him. And the woman prays. She spends days and nights down on her knees at some altar pleading and petitioning and believing.

"And he dies. Do you understand that? She is on her knees day and night and she talks with God about how much she loves her husband and needs him, but he dies. What is your explanation? Why didn't God listen to that woman?"

We can only tell him that we do not know; no one knows; that the ways of the Almighty Creator are beyond our knowing.

"But why does she pray to God at all," we ask, "if there were no affirmative answers to human prayers?

Why does she not pray on bended knees before the doctor if he's so wise?"

"She prayed to God. But who heard?"

"We cannot know all; we are not God. There may have been forces working against success in that prayer, forces we do not understand. There may have been lack of faith, channels blocked. We don't know. We do know that prayer does avail many times, when all other hope is gone."

"You're credulous."

"But these things have happened. And when they do happen—then what? When the prayer is answered, then what?"

A cry of pain comes out of the darkness. "O God," a woman pleads, "take away this pain. I will love you, God, if you will take this agony away. Dear God. . . ."

What about this agony of hers? The voices chatter with their questions. What about her pain? Who put it there? Why doesn't God take it away? Why does He let it exist at all?

These are the real cocktail-party questions. It is the casual social chitchat about faith that is not casual because it reflects a real desire to understand, but not a real desire always to search out answers.

At best we are only guessing. We do not know the answers, not factually, and there are many answers given, by assorted theologies, and some believe pain is only from the devil, and some say it is simply the workings of the laws; pain grows out of error and error grows only if we let it and when we have evolved fully enough as individual souls, there will be no pain.

But the voice pursues us; the answer is no answer. Give us one. Or else of what substance is your faith?

A thousand answers have been made without resolving the issue. It is God's punishment; when you suffer you are paying a penalty imposed by Heaven. The Christian Church once believed this so strongly that it called the use of anesthetics by physicians an invention of Satan to thwart the will of the Almighty.

Pain is punishment for sin, the church once declared, but now largely doubts. It is unreal and the product of wrong thinking, the Christian Scientist believes. It is God's will, the Jew declares. It is a way of teaching us, of warning us, of helping us to grow. It is a matter of germs and nerve vibrations, the doctor states.

The voices around us persist.

But the woman's voice is hushed; no cry of pain is heard. They say she is asleep. Physicians have given her an injection and she sleeps, and feels nothing. A moment ago she was in pain and now she rests because doctors have injected a substance into her body.

Not God, the voices cry. But a doctor.

And who made these doctors, and who gave them minds to understand and explore, and from where came the herbs and chemicals that when properly mixed soothe pain and heal?

If they do not come from God, then from where?

Wherever we turn, the voices and their questions pursue us. They are particularly sharp and bitter where they find faith strongest, primarily because they attempt to test faith by their own standards, as if they could mix their crude oil with holy water.

But if we had the certainty demanded in the questions that cry out of the dark, if we insisted only on materialistic certainty, we would have no faith and we would have no certainty either. We would, in fact, give up the certainty of faith for the uncertainty of the materialistic concept that is forever changing.

The challenge grows stronger. Some of the more entrenched and orthodox of the militant nonbelievers become greatly agitated. "All right, have your faith," their voices cry. "Live and die with your faith. We will still seek for solid things, for unequivocating answers, for reality. When we find God, we will record His full dimensions, down to the last millimeter of space."

"And where will your laboratory be then?"

"The universe. The whole universe."

"You will know everything, as Adam and Eve in the legend knew everything after they ate of the Tree of Knowledge, just before they were driven out of Eden?"

"We will run across the universe like children down a street." There is laughter in the voice. "Do we not know much already? The universe is matter. We have explored to the heart of the atom."

The voices grow louder and more certain. We have put wings upon ourselves and hurtled through the atmosphere. We have learned to transmit sound and image across space. We have conquered cold and heat, we have learned to seed the clouds with rain. Yes, we still have much to learn. But man and science are learning it, painstakingly, day by day, and without magic or make-believe or wishes or prayers. Is not all of that true?

"And what do you call matter?"

Silence. Then: "The substance of the universe, made up of atoms which in turn are made up of electrons and protons, forever in motion, like infinitesimal solar systems. At its heart, therefore, matter is energy in motion."

We ask, "What is energy?"

"It has many forms of expression. In all of them we find a common denominator: Energy is power, inherent and quiescent and dormant, or forcibly exerted."

Suddenly it has become topsy-turvy. The materialist talks not of substance, but of motion and energy and power.

All the solidity, all the substance of reality that we can touch and see and taste—all of it is, in effect, nonexistent; it dwindles on investigation to a collection of nothingnesses whirling around themselves, nothing chasing nothing in an endless array of solar systems, one within the other, a nest of universes, one inside the other, like an Oriental puzzle.

So they will build bigger and bigger telescopes to see farther and farther, and launch larger and larger rockets to reach deeper and deeper into space, and they will construct more powerful microscopes to see smaller and smaller particles of energy—and infinity will stretch out forever in both directions.

"And what is the ultimate source of this energy?" a voice asks.

"One day we will know."

The voice speaks with calm. Men have discovered much—yet the universe retreats before them. They have learned much about the material world and will go on learning more.

But is the essential truth they seek closer at hand than any dare admit?

For the "energy" they do not understand appears to be in everything that is, as far as the telescope and the test tube and the microscope have been able to penetrate.

We ask: "What is the weight of an average thought?"

The voices are silent.

"And which sense perceives the thought?"

No answer.

"And when will you have these answers? And do you believe your method will lead you to ultimate truth?"

There can be no answer, for they do not know.

"The Lord is my shepherd; I shall not want. . . ."

Who wrote these words? The Psalmist? Solomon himself? David? Whoever it was, whenever and under whatever circumstances, was very sure.

Where was his proof?

"Yea, though I walk through the valley of the shadow of death, I shall fear no evil: for thou art with me; thy rod and thy staff, they comfort me. . . ."

How is he so certain? How can his words have such power if they are mere naïve effusions? Whence comes this certainty that transmits itself to us over thousands of years as we read?

Is this not certainty that does not need to die unknowing, to wait for endless centuries to discover what may have been known from the beginning?

"Be still, and know that I am God."

However high we reach, the voices of doubt and confusion and disbelief and challenge will not be far distant.

But there are also other voices to be heard, voices

from distant lands and other times, voices that cry out with truth, even where they may speak with different words and other names.

Here is the Hindu god Krishna, in the Bhagavad-Gita:

"For I am the Creator of the universe—likewise am I the dissolution of the universe. Higher than I, there is naught. All the objects of the universe depend upon Me, and are sustained by Me. . . .

"Moisture in the water am I, O Prince of Pandu— light of the sun and moon am I, O Prince—the Sacred Syllable 'Aum'* in the Vedas am I, O Companion in the Chariot—the sound-waves in the air; the virility in men; the perfume of the earth; the glowing flame in the fire, am I, O Warrior of the Pandus. Yea, even the very life of all living things, am I, O Beloved. . . ."

Or a man named Brother Lawrence, one of great religious and spiritual force, writing in the seventeenth century:

"Let all our business be to know God; the more one *knows* Him, the more one *desires* to know Him. And as knowledge is commonly the measure of *love,* the deeper and more extensive our *knowledge* shall be, the greater will be our *love;* and if our love of God be great, we shall love Him equally in grief and in joy."

---

* Aum (also spelled Om) was originally a sacred word in the Hindu religion somewhat like the Christian-Judaic word Amen. It later came to stand for the Sacred Hindu Trinity, Brahma, Vishnu and Siva.

Or the voice of a Tibetan lama, writing in modern times, telling of his religion and beliefs and pointing out a great truth: "There *is* a God, a Supreme Being. What does it matter what we call Him? God is a fact. . . ."

There are voices against us, and voices for us, on the high levels of faith. There are metaphysical truths to be studied and explored; there is wisdom to be absorbed.

But there is one Voice that speaks with truth, Whose words reach our immortal lives and meaning, vibrant through space and time:

"Therefore whosoever heareth these sayings of mine, and doeth them, I will liken him unto a wise man, which built his house upon a rock:

"And the rain descended, and the floods came, and the winds blew, and beat upon that house; and it fell not: for it was founded upon a rock.

"And every one that heareth these sayings of mine, and doeth them not, shall be likened unto a foolish man which built his house upon the sand:

"And the rain descended, and the floods came, and the winds blew, and beat upon that house; and it fell: and great was the fall of it.

"And it came to pass, when Jesus had finished these sayings, the people were astonished at his doctrine:

"For he taught them as one having authority, and not as the scribes."

The air is still and the night is hushed.

A warmth sweeps through us that we have not experienced before.

We have a pervading sense of power that is of us and yet is not of us.

We have surrendered ourselves to something beyond ourselves, to the ultimate good, and in so doing we begin to be aware of the fulfillment of the spiritual Self within each of us, the realization of that Self in every aspect of our lives.

21

LOGOS

"In the beginning was the Word, and the Word was with God, and the Word was God.

"The same was in the beginning with God.

"All things were made by him; and without him was not any thing made that was made."

In the hush the winds die down and silence comes, silence that seems to reach out, alive and vibrating on every side.

We listen. A thousand of us, or ten thousand, or ten million. For each it is the same and for each it is individual, the music of silence, the intimation of the Presence.

Waiting, our thoughts run on, to others who sought. The ancient men of primitive tribes who raised strange idols: Stonehenge and its elusive meanings and implications reaching back to the predawn of civilized man. Or an ancient Roman, bowing before his household god to ask a minor favor. Or early

Christians in their hidden places, carrying candles and flickering oil lamps in the bone-littered hush of cata-combs. The king-worshipers and tree-worshipers and animal-worshipers, and Moses smashing the tablets of the Ten Commandments because his people bowed before a Golden Calf.

So often we listen, and so often we do not understand.

Beyond us are the words and the ideas and the meanings, beyond us and around us, and they drift in on winds we cannot wholly know.

"In the beginning was the Word," declares St. John, "and the Word was with God, and the Word was God.

"The same was in the beginning with God.

"All things were made by him; and without him was not any thing made that was made.

"In him was life; and the life was the light of men.

"And the light shineth in darkness; and the darkness comprehended it not."

Who is meant by the Word?

The Greek term is "Logos."

This is the word found in many places in the Bible, as here in John.

It has several meanings and interpretations. It can be translated as "the word," or as "reason," as "wisdom" or "science." We find its transmutation in modern words that end in "ology"—biology, geology, psychology and the like, where the root meaning implies study, knowledge, science.

But "Logos" has another and deeper implication: it has the meaning of Deity Itself. This is seen in our own Bible in several ways. In certain Biblical passages it assumes the meaning of the "word of God," as spoken by His prophets. In certain passages, notably in the Proverbs, the Word itself is personified and speaks, bidding mankind to love wisdom and right for its own sake, and to shun wickedness as an abomination.

Throughout the Bible there are instances in which the Lord speaks to man, in which His word is revealed through His prophets. Throughout the New Testament we have the added concept of the Logos, the Word made manifest, incarnate, through Jesus.

The Logos is God. It is God speaking to us in the silence; it is His word, carried on the winds; it is the breath of the night and the scent of the forest and the brine of the sea.

Out of the darkness around us, out of the aloneness of our thought and meditation, the words swirl in upon us, out of our lives, out of the corners of our soul, out of a thousand forgotten classrooms and episodes and childish searchings:

"Thus saith the Lord the King of Israel, and his redeemer the Lord of hosts; I am the first, and I am the last; and beside me there is no God. . . .

"Fear ye not, neither be afraid: have not I told

thee from that time, and have declared it? ye are even my witnesses. Is there a God beside me? yea, there is no God; I know not any.

"They that make a graven image are all of them vanity . . ."

Out of the darkness and silence, out of despair and defeat, out of frustration and loneliness and rejection and emptiness, out of scorn, out of trying and failing and trying once again, out of the need for strength, out of weakness admitted, out of our foolishness and misunderstanding and groping and yearning—out of all the things for which we sometimes think ourselves guilty and sometimes not, we inwardly seek and find the Word, at once immediate and personal and all-encompassing.

"Then the Lord answered Job out of the whirlwind, and said,

"Who is this that darkeneth counsel by words without knowledge?

"Gird up thy loins like a man; for I will demand of thee, and answer thou me.

"Where wast thou when I laid the foundations of the earth? Declare, if thou hast understanding.

"Who hath laid the measures thereof, if thou knowest? or who hath stretched the line upon it? . . .

"Hath the rain a father? or who hath begotten the drops of dew?

"Out of whose womb came the ice? and the hoary frost of heaven, who hath gendered it?

"The waters are hid as with a stone, and the face of the deep is frozen.

"Canst thou bind the sweet influences of Pleiades, or loose the bands of Orion?

"Canst thou bring forth Mazzaroth in his season? or canst thou guide Arcturus with his sons?

"Knowest thou the ordinances of heaven? canst thou set the dominion thereof in the earth? . . ."

Bits and fragments we have learned, but dominion we have not. And the more we learn, the more elusive that dominion seems.

Out of our darkness comes the meaning and the Word that is not elusive, for it waits upon us and our willingness to understand.

"And when thou prayest," Jesus told His followers, gathered before Him for the Sermon, "thou shalt not be as the hypocrites are: for they love to pray standing in the synagogues and in the corners of the streets, that they may be seen of men. Verily I say unto you, They have their reward."

"But thou, when thou prayest, enter into thy closet, and when thou hast shut thy door, pray to thy Father which is in secret; and thy Father which seeth in secret shall reward thee openly.

"But when ye pray, use not vain repetitions, as the heathen do: for they think that they shall be heard for their much speaking.

"Be not ye therefore like unto them: for your

Father knoweth what things ye have need of, before ye ask him."

Your Father knoweth. Your Father which is in secret.

Here in the darkness that is our secret place, our private place of prayer, we remember these words. Here in secret, we seek to learn to listen and to grasp meaning.

And understanding flows in upon us and we know that faith is no single thing, but many things; no one word or set of promises and practices, but many words and many promises that must be pledged and kept.

Faith is the blended pattern of our lives, the lights and shadows of our existence; it is what we do, what we say, what we think, what we are; each of these is a garment of our faith. Every action we make, every breath we dare to draw, is a decision about the universe.

The knowledge sweeps upon us with overwhelming force.

The Word is with us in this secret place, if we but learn to listen.

This is the Logos, the wordless word, the living, throbbing, breathing silence of wonder.

"Be still, and know that I am God."

22

SUMMIT

The spur of naked rock curves like a scimitar upward to the peak.

Our goal now is only a little distance beyond us, almost within our grasp.

The achievement of this goal is a victory involving unusual implications.

It is quite personal, because it is the individual in relationship to the cosmos.

It is personal because it is our acceptance, our submission, our need and our fulfillment.

We do, indeed, make a decision, here in this lonely outpost of ourselves.

And each one is alone, and each is part of the whole and each finds his own truth.

The meaning of what Jesus taught to the poor and oppressed in an obscure community of the Mideast some two thousand years ago comes to us not as dogma or theology, but in its simplest application.

He was the Teacher, the Master, the Wayshower, the Forgiver.

For twenty centuries, millions have been repeating his message, believing it in a measure, practicing it in a measure, rejecting it also, sometimes even as they speak the words of their belief, yet still striving toward the ideals at the core.

The Christian faith is a faith in the miraculous; if we do not believe in miracles, we do not believe in Him.

Did the palsied man arise? Was the man with the withered hand made whole? Was the lady with the flow of blood healed by touching His garment? Did Lazarus actually come forth from the tomb?

We must believe or not believe, accept or not accept; there is no room for any middle ground of half belief or half doubt.

It was a mere two thousand years ago, all of this —in geological terms it is an infinitesimal fraction of a second in time. Humanity has been hundreds of thousands of years in development; it has changed little in these two thousand years. The intelligence of many in that time, especially in the lands around the Mediterranean, in many instances equalled or excelled that of our own day.

It happened or it did not.

A child was born in a stable, and wise men came there, to kneel before the Child, and bring Him gifts, because He was the anointed Child of God, and angels sang in the heavens. . . .

And when He was a man, there was such love and power and compassion in Him that His touch or word healed the sick and raised the dead. . . .

And He taught that we should have love for each other, for our enemies, and compassion and forgiveness.

He told us to be perfect, even as our Father which is in Heaven is perfect.

He taught throughout the land and in the temples, and the wisest scholars of that day tempted Him with shrewd questions and He answered them all. When one questioner remarked discreetly that Jesus spoke the truth, the Master told him, "Thou are not far from the kingdom of God."

And when He had answered this way, according to the gospel of St. Mark, the Pharisees and Herodians left off their attempts because "no man durst ask him any question."

He was part of the tableau that had been foretold, the drama of humanity and its weakness, of betrayal by His friend and disciple. He was tried before a tribune of orthodoxy and the technocrats of the soul, bartered to a mob by a politician who thought truth was a slightly amusing joke, dragged through humiliation and derision and agony by ignorance and callousness and taunting incredulity, and in the midst of agony He called out, "Father, forgive them . . ."

How deep is such love, that it pleads even for its tormentors and would-be destroyers in their hour?

Already He had told His disciples: "Peace I leave with you, my peace I give unto you: not as the world giveth, give I unto you. Let not your heart be troubled, neither let it be afraid. . . .

"As the Father hath loved me, so have I loved you: continue ye in my love.

"If ye keep my commandments, ye shall abide in my love; even as I have kept my Father's commandments, and abide in his love.

"These things have I spoken unto you, that my joy might remain in you, and that your joy might be full.

"This is my commandment, That ye love one another, as I have loved you.

"Greater love hath no man than this, that a man lay down his life for his friends.

"Ye are my friends, if ye do whatsoever I command . . ."

He brought us the Word of God, and was condemned and was nailed to a Cross and in His agony He loved and forgave and asked God's forgiveness for His enemies.

This was the reality.

And if His is not the way and the truth, there can be no way and there is no truth.

Beneath the stars there is a wave of emptiness and silence and infinite sadness; it is a cold, quiet wordless thing, as if all the universe had paused in its tracks, and held its breath.

The King has died. The King has been taken down from the Cross and carried to the tomb and a stone and guards have been placed before it. And these are the saddest days of the people of the world, days of silence and emptiness.

If this thing had happened so, and nothing more, what would it have meant?

A Sunday morning—an early Sunday morning—remained.

Centuries later, to live again that Sunday morning when the two Marys went to the tomb and found the stone rolled away and the sepulcher empty, we go to church.

It is early morning, shortly after seven, yet the church is thronged, the altar decorated with flowers; there is a sense of freshness and newness and beauty.

This is the day we celebrate, when we bedeck ourselves in our finest, and churchmen wear their brightest robes, and the choir sings Hallelujah, hallelujah, hallelujah—Christ is risen. The Lord is risen.

Morning sun spills through the stained glass and throws bright colors on the altar and the flowers, the white robes of the minister and his assistants and the choir, lighting the whole church with its glow.

Christ is risen, the voices cry out. Our Lord is risen. The tomb is empty.

And in the center some young man in a white cassock holds up a golden cross.

"Christ is risen!" the voices cry.

The sun glitters on the gold.

It is emotion, beauty, poetry—and truth.

"I am the way, the truth and the life," He told us. Did it happen? And did it happen in this way, as it is recorded?

And in what other way could it have happened but in the way it is told? Man being man, it had to happen this way.

They nailed Truth to a Cross, truth personified in the Christ; they jeered and spat and ridiculed Him and His love and His Kingdom, and cried out against Him, but He did not die and Truth did not die.

And He arose from the dead, and ascended into Heaven, to be at the side of God the Father Almighty, Maker of the Heavens and the Earth.

This is our faith.

It is the high summit of faith for the world.

For there are many ways but only one way, and many roads but only one and many truths but only one.

And the Father is one, and the Son.

§ 222 §

SUMMIT

And in His death, all died and in His life all live.

The upward slope is gentle and the distance is not far. The mist is golden and the world is a patchwork of beauty at our feet and the winds are cool against our cheek.

Unshackled, we run to our summit height.